Primary Source Readings in
Catholic Church History

Primary Source Readings in
Catholic Church History

Robert Feduccia Jr.
with Nick Wagner

saint mary's press

The publishing team included Robert Feduccia Jr., development editor; Louis Yock, HED, consultant; Lorraine Kilmartin, reviewer; Mary Koehler, permissions editor; Craig Aurness/CORBIS and PhotoDisc, Inc., cover images; prepress and manufacturing coordinated by the prepublication and production services departments of Saint Mary's Press.

Printed in the United States of America

1328

ISBN 978-0-88489-868-9

Library of Congress Cataloging-in-Publication Data

Feduccia, Robert.
    Primary source readings in Catholic Church history / Robert Feduccia, Jr. with Nick Wagner.
        p. cm.
    Includes index.
    ISBN 978-0-88489-868-9 (pbk.)
        1. Catholic Church—History—Sources. I. Wagner, Nick, 1957–
II. Title.
BX945.3.F44 2005
282'.09—dc22

                                                            2005000786

Contents

Looking through old pictures of ourselves is always fun. In those dated photos, we see what we looked like when we were born; we remember early birthdays and laugh about some of the presents we received; and perhaps we look at some pictures with embarrassment. Clothing, hairstyles, and old boyfriends or girlfriends have the potential to ruin the pictures in a family album. Hairstyles come and go. Clothing styles change quickly. But the pictures are an undeniable testament to what or who we thought was cool. They are more than just static images. They reveal a little about our thoughts, our feelings, and our attitudes.

Pictures are a frozen moment in time. Life is continuous, and because of that, we hardly notice the changes happening to us. A student looks at herself every day in the mirror and probably doesn't notice any change in her appearance. But if that student compares her eighth-grade picture to her ninth-grade picture, the changes are obvious, if not dramatic. This book, *Primary Source Readings in Catholic Church History*, is like the Church's family photo album, filled with snapshots—frozen moments in time.

In this book, you will find pictures of the Church's birth, the hard times she has suffered, and the infusion of new life in every age. The Church's album also includes pictures of family fights. West versus East, emperor versus pope, and reformers versus counter-reformers are fights that stand in portrait. Yet, when we place those frozen moments in time next to each other, a mosaic appears. In this composite picture you find heroic people who love the Lord and who want to be his servants. You also find that Jesus's words from Matthew 16:18 and from Matthew 28:20 are true: "I will build my church, and the gates of Hades will not prevail against it," and "Remember, I am with you always, to the end of the age."

These snapshots are not just about humans and humanity's attempt to steer the Church on the right course. They are also a story of God. Every letter, document, and report is also a picture of God: Father, Son, and Holy Spirit. In them, God reaches out to humans in love and calls humanity into an intimate relationship. Although the Church changes from century to century, God does not. God is constant and continuously reaches out to humanity and touches human hearts. The great Catholic thinker Edward Schillebeeckx once wrote: "God's saving activity 'makes history' by revealing itself, and it reveals itself by becoming history." The snapshots in this book reveal the Church's history. But they also tell the story of God's constant love and desire to draw humanity into a deeper relationship with him.

Chapter 1

Initiation into a Community:
The Body of Christ as a Model of the Church

"A Rite of Passage"

Who Wrote It?

Rev. Aidan Kavanagh, OSB, was born in 1929 in Mexia, Texas. He became a Benedictine monk of Saint Meinrad Archabbey, Saint Meinrad, Indiana, in 1952 and was ordained to the priesthood in 1957. Kavanagh taught at Saint Meinrad School of Theology and also at the University of Notre Dame, where he was the director of graduate studies in liturgy and theology. In 1974, he joined the faculty at Yale Divinity School as a professor of liturgics.

When Was It Written?

"A Rite of Passage" was delivered as part of a lecture at the Theology Institute at Holy Cross Abbey in Canon City, Colorado, in 1977.

Why Was It Written?

For many years, Rev. Aidan Kavanagh has championed a renewal in the way sacraments are celebrated. In particular, he has worked to enliven the rites of initiation, the way people come into the Church. He believes that enlivening these rites can happen by restoring the practices of the early Christian communities. He wants today's Church to celebrate a person's entrance into the Body of Christ in much the same way the early Christians brought people into the community of faith. To try to influence such changes, he has written many scholarly books on the initiation practices of the early Christians. His academic writings are well respected and influential. But Kavanagh wanted to accomplish something that scholarly essays could not. He wanted a story to bring to life in clear imagery, the sounds, smells, and richness of the early Christian initiation.

Why Is It Still Important Today?

In many places, the sacred Scriptures refer to the Church as the Body of Christ. To highlight this dimension, or model, of the Church, one emphasizes the Church as a community bound together by the Holy Spirit. This unity is expressed in the way the community speaks about or professes its faith, in the way it worships and celebrates, and in the way its members foster companionship with one another. "A Rite of Passage" demonstrates all these aspects and can illumine the Body of Christ as a model for the Church.

Primary Source: "A Rite of Passage"

I have always rather liked the gruff robustness of the first rubric for baptism found in a late fourth-century church order which directs that the bishop enter the vestibule of the baptistery and say to the catechumens without commentary or apology only four words: "Take off your clothes." There is no evidence that the assistants fainted or the catechumens asked what he meant. Catechesis and much prayer and fasting had led them to understand that the language of their passage this night in Christ from death to life would be the language of the bathhouse and the tomb—not that of the forum and the drawing room.

So they stripped and stood there, probably, faint from fasting, shivering from the cold of early Easter morning and with awe at what was about to transpire. Years of formation were about to be consummated; years of having their motives and lives scrutinized; years of hearing the word of God read and expounded at worship; years of being dismissed with prayer before the Faithful went on to celebrate the eucharist; years of having the doors to the assembly hall closed to them; years of seeing the tomb-like baptistery building only from without; years of hearing the old folks of the community tell hair-raising tales of what being a Christian had cost their own grandparents when the emperors were still pagan; years of running into a reticent and reverent vagueness concerning what was actually done by the Faithful at the breaking of bread and in that closed baptistery. . . . Tonight all this was about to end as they stood here naked on a cold floor in the gloom of this eerie room.

Abruptly the bishop demands that they face westward, toward where the sun dies swallowed up in darkness, and denounce the King of shadows and death and things that go bump in the night. Each one of them comes forward to do this loudly under the hooded gaze of the bishop (who is tired from presiding all night at the vigil continuing next door in the church), as deacons shield the nudity of the male catechumens from the women, and deaconesses screen the women in the same manner. This is when each of them finally lets go of the world and of life as they have known it: the umbilical cord is cut, but they have not yet begun to breathe.

Deaconesses

Deaconesses were women who had important roles in the early Church. Bishop, priest, and deacon are ministries in the Church to which men are ordained. Although history does not indicate that deaconesses were ordained, the role of deaconesses and their significance in the life of the Christian community is evident. They led women in prayer; they served the community's widows; and they assisted in the Baptism of women.

Then they must each turn eastwards toward where the sun surges up bathed in a light which just now can be seen stealing into the alabaster windows of the room. They must voice their acceptance of the King of light and life who has trampled down death by his own death. As each one finishes this he or she is fallen upon by a deacon or a deaconess who vigorously rubs olive oil into his or her body, as the bishop perhaps dozes off briefly, leaning on his cane. (He is like an old surgeon waiting for the operation to begin.)

When all the catechumens have been thoroughly oiled, they and the bishop are suddenly startled by the crash of the baptistery doors being thrown open. Brilliant golden light spills out into the shadowy vestibule, and following the bishop (who has now regained his composure) the catechumens and the assistant presbyters, deacons, deaconesses, and sponsors move into the most glorious room most of them have ever seen. It is a high, arbor-like pavilion of green, gold, purple, and white mosaic from marble floor to domed ceiling sparkling like jewels in the light of innumerable oil lamps that fill the room with a heady warmth. The windows are beginning to blaze with the light of Easter dawn. The walls curl with vines and tendrils that thrust up from the floor, and at their tops apostles gaze down robed in snow-white togas, holding crowns. They stand around a golden chair draped with purple upon which rests only an open book. And above all these, in the highest point of the ballooning dome, a naked Jesus (very much in the flesh) stands up to his waist in the Jordan as an unkempt John pours water on him and God's disembodied hand points the Holy Spirit at Jesus' head in the form of a white bird.

Suddenly the catechumens realize that they have unconsciously formed themselves into a mirror-image of this lofty icon on the floor directly beneath it. They are standing around a pool let into the middle of the floor, into which gushes water pouring noisily from the mouth of a stone lion crouching atop a pillar at poolside. The bishop stands beside this, his presbyters on each side: a deacon has entered the pool, and the other assistants are trying to maintain a modicum of decorum among the catechumens who forget their nakedness as they crowd close to see. The room is warm, humid, and it glows. It is a golden paradise in a bathhouse in a mausoleum: an oasis, Eden restored: the navel of the world, where death and life meet, copulate, and become undistinguishable from each other. Jonah peers out from a niche, Noah from another, Moses from a third, and the paralytic carrying his stretcher from a fourth. The windows begin to sweat.

The bishop rumbles a massive prayer—something about the Spirit and the waters of life and death—and then pokes the water a few times with his cane. The catechumens recall Moses doing something like that to a rock from which water flowed, and they are mightily impressed. Then a young male catechumen of about ten, the son of pious parents, is led down into the pool by the deacon. The water is warm (it has been heated in a furnace), and the oil on his body spreads out on the surface in iridescent swirls. The deacon positions the child near the cascade from the lion's mouth. The bishop leans over on his cane, and in a voice that sounds like something out of the Apocalypse, says: "Euphemius! Do you believe in God the Father, who created all of heaven and earth?" After a nudge from the deacon beside him, the boy murmurs that he does. And just in time, for the deacon, who has been doing this for fifty years and is the boy's grandfather, wraps him in his arms, lifts him backwards into the rushing water and forces him under the surface. The old deacon smiles through his beard at the wide brown eyes that look up at him in shock and fear from beneath the water (the boy has purposely not been told what to expect). Then he raises him up coughing and sputtering. The bishop waits until he can speak again, and leaning over a second time, tapping the boy on the shoulder with his cane, says: "Euphemius! Do you believe in Jesus Christ, God's only Son, who was conceived of the Virgin Mary, suffered under Pontius Pilate, and was crucified, died, and was buried? Who rose on the third day and ascended into heaven, from whence he will come again to judge the living and the dead?" This time he replies like a shot, "I do," and then holds his nose. . . . "Euphemius! Do you believe in the Holy Spirit, the master and giver of life, who proceeds from the Father, who is to be honored and glorified equally with the Father and the Son, who spoke by the Prophets? And in one holy, catholic, and apostolic Church which is the communion of God's holy ones? And in the life that is coming?" "I do."

When he comes up the third time, his vast grandfather gathers him in his arms and carries him up the steps leading out of the pool. There another deacon roughly dries Euphemius with a warm towel, and a senior presbyter, who is almost ninety and is regarded by all as a "confessor" because he was imprisoned for the faith as a young man, tremulously pours perfumed oil from a glass pitcher over the boy's damp head until it soaks his hair and runs down over his upper body. The fragrance of this enormously expensive oil fills the room as the old man mutters: "God's servant, Euphemius, is anointed in the name of the Father, Son, and Holy Spirit." Euphemius is then wrapped in a new linen tunic; the fragrant chrism seeps into it, and he is given a burning terracotta oil lamp and told to go stand by the door and keep quiet. Meanwhile, the other baptisms have continued.

When all have been done in this same manner (an old deaconess, a widow, replaced Euphemius's grandfather when it came the women's time), the clergy strike up the Easter hymn, "Christ is risen from the dead, he has crushed death by his death and bestowed life on those who lay in the tomb." To this constantly repeated melody interspersed with the Psalm verse, "Let God arise and smite his enemies," the whole baptismal party—tired, damp, thrilled, and oily—walk out into the blaze of Easter morning and go next door to the church led by the bishop. There he bangs on the closed doors with his cane: they are flung open, the endless vigil is halted, and the baptismal party enters as all take up the hymn, "Christ is risen . . . ," which is all but drowned out by the ovations that greet Christ truly risen in his newly-born ones. As they enter, the fragrance of chrism fills the church: it is the Easter-smell, God's grace olfactorally incarnate. The pious struggle to get near the newly baptized to touch their chrismed hair and rub its fragrance on their own faces. All is chaos until the baptismal party manages to reach the towering ambo that stands in the middle of the pewless hall. The bishop ascends its lower front steps, turns to face the white-clad neophytes grouped at the bottom with their burning lamps and the boisterous faithful now held back by a phalanx of well-built acolytes and doorkeepers. Euphemius's mother has fainted and been carried outside for some air.

The bishop opens his arms to the neophytes and once again all burst into "Christ is risen," *Christos aneste. . . .* He then affirms and seals their baptism after prayer, for all the Faithful to see, with an au-thoritative gesture of paternity—laying his hand on each head, signing each oily forehead once again in the form of a cross, while booming out: "The servant of God is sealed with the Holy Spirit." To which all reply in a thunderous "Amen," and for the first time the former cate-chumens receive and give the kiss of peace. Everyone is in tears.

While this continues, bread and wine are laid out on the holy table; the bishop then prays at great length over them after things quiet down, and the neophytes lead all to communion with Euphemius out in front. While his grandfather holds his lamp, Euphemius dines on the precious Body whose true and undoubted member he has become; drinks the precious Blood of him in whom he himself has now died; and just this once drinks from two other special cups—one containing baptismal water, the other containing milk and honey mixed as a gustatory icon of the promised land into which he and his colleagues have finally entered out of the desert through Jordan's waters. Then his mother (now recovered and somewhat pale, still insisting she had only stumbled) took him home and put him, fragrantly, to bed.

Euphemius had come a long way. He had passed from death into a life he lives still.

Chapter 2

The Ship of Salvation:
The Church as an Institution

"The Dream of Saint John Bosco"

Who Wrote It?

Saint John Bosco lived in the northern Italian city of Turin during the 1840s. Grieved by the poverty and the crime among urban young people, he dedicated his ministry to the young people. He sheltered countless numbers of the city's homeless young people and instructed them in the Catholic faith. Because of his tireless and selfless dedication to the young people of Turin, Bosco has been named the patron saint of those who work with young people.

When Was It Written?

When Saint John Bosco had his dream is not known. But on May 30, 1862, he told the boys he was sheltering that he had a good story for them. This chapter contains the allegory he told them.

Why Was It Written?

Workers in the new factories being built endured long work hours for very little money. Because of those working conditions, the young people of the city were left poor and unsupervised. Those desperate young people turned to robbery and other crimes to make a way for their survival. The situation was in dire need of the good news of Jesus

Christ. Scholars agree that Saint John Bosco had simple reasons for telling the dream. Those reasons were that he wanted the boys to stay close to the Church, to pray for the Holy Father, and to hold on to a love for Mary and the Blessed Sacrament. During Bosco's time, a ship at sea was a common analogy for the Church. The secular world was seen as waves and storms that could swallow and drown the earth's peoples. In order to be saved from such danger, a person had to band together with others on a sturdy ship with a noble and trustworthy captain.

Why Is It Still Important Today?

Very shortly after Saint John Bosco told the dream to the boys, they began to discuss what it could mean. Some felt it was simply an allegory. Others believed that it was a prophecy or a vision of the future. The dream remains important today for many reasons. Certainly, Bosco's reason for telling the dream to that group of boys remains. But for the purposes of this book, "The Dream of Saint John Bosco" provides a rich image for a model of the Church as an institution. Among the many ways of understanding what the Church and its purpose are, seeing the Church as an institution provides Catholics with clarity and certainty. Such surety can provide comfort during times such as these when many discomforting events are taking place.

Primary Source: "The Dream of Saint John Bosco"

A few nights ago I had a dream. True, dreams are nothing but dreams, but still I'll tell it to you for your spiritual benefit, just as I would tell you even my sins—only I'm afraid I'd send you scurrying away before the roof fell in. Try to picture yourselves with me on the seashore, or, better still, on an outlying cliff with no other land in sight. The vast expanse of water is covered with a formidable array of ships in battle formation, prows fitted with sharp, spearlike beaks capable of breaking through any defense. All are heavily armed with cannons, incendiary bombs, and firearms of all sorts—even books—and are heading toward one stately ship, mightier than them all. As they close in, they try to ram it, set it afire, and cripple it as much as possible.

This stately vessel is shielded by a flotilla escort. Winds and waves are with the enemy. In the midst of this endless sea, two solid columns, a short distance apart, soar high into the sky: one is surmounted by a statue of the Immaculate Virgin at whose feet a large inscription reads: *Help of Christians;* the other, far loftier and sturdier, supports a Host of proportionate size and bears beneath it the inscription *Salvation of believers.*

The flagship commander—the Roman Pontiff—seeing the enemy's fury and his auxiliary ships' very grave predicament, summons his captains to a conference. However, as they discuss their strategy, a furious storm breaks out and they must return to their ships.

When the storm abates, the Pope again summons his captains as the flagship keeps on its course. But the storm rages again. Standing at the helm, the Pope strains every muscle to steer his ship between the two columns from whose summits hang many anchors and strong hooks linked to chains.

The entire enemy fleet closes in to intercept and sink the flagship at all costs. They bombard it with everything they have: books and pamphlets, incendiary bombs, firearms, cannons. The battle rages ever more furious. Beaked prows ram the flagship again and again, but to no avail, as, unscathed and undaunted, it keeps on its course. At times a formidable ram splinters a gaping hole into its hull, but, immediately, a breeze from the two columns instantly seals the gash.

Meanwhile, enemy cannons blow up, firearms and beaks fall to pieces, ships crack up and sink to the bottom. In blind fury the enemy takes to hand-to-hand combat, cursing and blaspheming. Suddenly the Pope falls, seriously wounded. He is instantly helped up but, struck down a second time, dies. A shout of victory rises from the enemy and wild rejoicing sweeps their ships. But no sooner is the Pope dead than another takes his place. The captains of the auxiliary ships elected him so quickly that the news of the Pope's death coincides with that of his successor's election. The enemy's self-assurance wanes.

Breaking through all resistance, the new Pope steers his ship safely between the two columns and moors it to the two columns; first, to the one surmounted by the Host, and then to the other, topped by the statue of the Virgin. At this point, something unexpected happens. The enemy ships panic and disperse, colliding with and scuttling each other.

Some auxiliary ships which had gallantly fought alongside their flagship are the first to tie up at the two columns. Many others, which had fearfully kept far away from the fight, stand still, cautiously waiting until the wrecked enemy ships vanish under the waves. Then, they too head for the two columns, tie up at the swinging hooks, and ride safe and tranquil beside their flagship. A great calm now covers the sea.

"And so," Don Bosco at this point asked Father Rua, "what do you make of this?"

"I think," he answered, "that the flagship symbolizes the Church commanded by the Pope; the ships represent mankind; the sea is an image of the world. The flagship's defenders are the laity loyal to the Church; the attackers are her enemies who strive with every weapon to destroy her. The two columns, I'd say, symbolize devotion to Mary and the Blessed Sacrament."

Father Rua did not mention the Pope who fell and died. Don Bosco, too, kept silent on this point, simply adding: "Very well, Father, except for one thing: the enemy ships symbolize persecutions. Very grave trials await the Church. What we suffered so far is almost nothing compared to what is going to happen. The enemies of the Church are symbolized by the ships which strive their utmost to sink the flagship. Only two things can save us in such a grave hour: devotion to Mary and frequent Communion. Let's do our very best to use these two means and have others use them everywhere. Good night!"

Chapter 3

The Descent of the Holy Spirit:
The Church Is Revealed

Acts of the Apostles 2:1–42

Who Wrote It?

Saint Luke the Evangelist wrote the Acts of the Apostles. Luke lived at the same time as many of Jesus's followers, but he was different from most of them. First, he was not one of the original disciples. Second, he was a Gentile—someone who was not a Jew. Third, he was not from Galilee or Jerusalem. He is believed to have been from Antioch, a city located about 275 miles north of Jerusalem on the Mediterranean Sea. Tradition holds that he was a doctor, and we know from his writings that he had a strong commitment to justice for those who were ill, and for all outsiders.

When Was It Written?

Most Catholic Scripture scholars believe that the Acts of the Apostles was written between AD 70 and AD 90.

Why Was It Written?

Saint Luke wrote two books of the Bible: the Gospel of Luke and the Acts of the Apostles. These two books are intended to be read together as a single story of God's action among his people. Luke wanted to explain how God's ancient promise of salvation is fulfilled in Jesus and continues to be fulfilled by a Church now enlivened with God's Holy Spirit. The reading in this chapter tells of the day of Pentecost, the birthday of the Church.

The ancient Israelites believed that they were chosen by God for salvation. But Luke's story says the promise of salvation is now given to people "from every nation under heaven" (Acts 2:5). In the story of the Pentecost, and throughout his writings, Luke intended to show that Jesus had extended God's promise of salvation to Gentiles, those who might be considered outsiders like him. The Spirit-filled Church had announced the promise of salvation to all parts and all peoples of the world. Jesus made the way for salvation and the Church preaches the way of salvation.

In the first verse of the first chapter of his Gospel, Luke tells us that he wants to provide the reader with an "orderly account." He seems to be saying that he wants to write a good story. He also wanted to show a connection between Jesus's work and the Church's mission.

We will read of the Holy Spirit's descent on the disciples at Pentecost and will see its similarity to the Gospel story of the Holy Spirit's descent upon Jesus at his baptism. Also, the Apostles healed the sick as Jesus did. The Apostles announced the message of Jesus and were rejected just as Jesus was. Luke seems to be saying that whatever happened to Jesus would happen to the Church. It could also be said that the way God acted in the life of Jesus is the way God will act in the life of the Church. Luke's story of Pentecost and the empowerment of the Church with the Holy Spirit is not a news report or an historical record but a rallying cry to summon the believers in Christ to continue the work of Christ by the power of the Holy Spirit.

Why Is It Still Important Today?

To benefit fully from the story of Pentecost, read it as something that is happening right now, not as something that happened long ago. God's promise of salvation is still being extended to all people, even to the outsiders.

When Luke wrote about Saint Peter's announcement of the "last days," he probably knew, just as we do, that there would be many more "days" after he was gone. But, as a doctor, Luke knew that every day is the last day for those who have no hope. In that sense, the days Luke lived in and the days you and I live in are the "last days." These are the days God has given to proclaim salvation to those who are oppressed. Other days may come, but *these* are the days, right now, for people to hear about God's salvation in Jesus. Dreams of justice and freedom are for everyone, especially for those who are defenseless or who cannot provide for themselves. Today is the day for everyone to have enough to eat and a place to live. God has promised salvation to every generation. This story remains important because there are still people, especially those on the outside of society's margins, who have not heard about or experienced God's promise.

Primary Source: Acts of the Apostles 2:1–42

When the day of Pentecost had come, they were all together in one place. And suddenly from heaven there came a sound like the rush of a violent wind, and it filled the entire house where they were sitting. Divided tongues, as of fire, appeared among them, and a tongue rested on each of them. All of them were filled with the Holy Spirit and began to speak in other languages, as the Spirit gave them ability.

Now there were devout Jews from every nation under heaven living in Jerusalem. And at this sound the crowd gathered and was bewildered, because each one heard them speaking in the native language of each. Amazed and astonished, they asked, "Are not all these who are speaking Galileans? And how is it that we hear, each of us, in our own native language? Parthians, Medes, Elamites, and residents of Mesopotamia, Judea and Cappadocia, Pontus and Asia, Phrygia and Pamphylia, Egypt and the parts of Libya belonging to Cyrene, and visitors from Rome, both Jews and proselytes, Cretans and Arabs—in our

Many Languages

Genesis 11 holds another story about languages—the story of the tower of Babel. This chapter from the Bible's first book tells about a time when all earth's peoples were one and spoke a single language. But because of the arrogance of the human race, the Lord confused their plans to build a tower to the heavens by confusing their language. The revelation of the Church at Pentecost shows that the Holy Spirit will unify the earth's peoples once again, despite the diversity of language.

own languages we hear them speaking about God's deeds of power." All were amazed and perplexed, saying to one another, "What does this mean?" But others sneered and said, "They are filled with new wine."

New Wine

Saint Luke used the term *new wine* only one other time. In Luke 5:37–39, Jesus tells the parable of the new wine and wineskin. In this parable, Jesus tells the disciples that an old wineskin cannot hold new wine. Rather, a new wineskin must hold new wine. In Acts 2:13, those who sneer at the disciples' new language abilities say the Apostles were drunk—"filled with new wine." Although they mocked the event, their statement was right. New wine—the outpouring of the Holy Spirit—was filling a new wineskin—the newly revealed Church.

But Peter, standing with the eleven, raised his voice and addressed them, "Men of Judea and all who live in Jerusalem, let this be known to you, and listen to what I say. Indeed, these are not drunk, as you suppose, for it is only nine o'clock in the morning. No, this is what was spoken through the prophet Joel:

'In the last days it will be, God
    declares,
that I will pour out my Spirit upon
    all flesh,
    and your sons and your
        daughters shall prophesy,
and your young men shall see
    visions
    and your old men shall dream
        dreams.
Even upon my slaves, both men
    and women,
    in those days I will pour out
        my Spirit;
    and they shall prophesy.
And I will show portents in the heaven above
    and signs on the earth below,
        blood, and fire, and smoky mist.
The sun shall be turned to darkness
    and the moon to blood,
        before the coming of the Lord's great and glorious day.
Then everyone who calls on the name of the Lord shall be saved.'

"You that are Israelites, listen to what I have to say: Jesus of Nazareth, a man attested to you by God with deeds of power, wonders, and signs that God did through him among you, as you yourselves know—this man, handed over to you according to the definite plan and foreknowledge of God, you crucified and killed by the hands of those outside the law. But God raised him up, having freed him from death, because it was impossible for him to be held in its power. For David says concerning him,

'I saw the Lord always before me,
for he is at my right hand so that I will not be shaken;
therefore my heart was glad, and my tongue rejoiced;
moreover my flesh will live in hope.
For you will not abandon my soul to Hades,
or let your Holy One experience corruption.
You have made known to me the ways of life;
you will make me full of gladness with your presence.'

"Fellow Israelites, I may say to you confidently of our ancestor David that he both died and was buried, and his tomb is with us to this day. Since he was a prophet, he knew that God had sworn with an oath to him that he would put one of his descendants on his throne. Foreseeing this, David spoke of the resurrection of the Messiah, saying,

'He was not abandoned to Hades,
nor did his flesh experience
corruption.'

This Jesus God raised up, and of that all of us are witnesses. Being therefore exalted at the right hand of God, and having received from the Father the promise of the Holy Spirit, he has poured out this that you both see and hear. For David did not ascend into the heavens, but he himself says,

'The Lord said to my Lord,
"Sit at my right hand,
until I make your enemies your
footstool."'

Therefore let the entire house of Israel know with certainty that God has made him both Lord and Messiah, this Jesus whom you crucified."

Now when they heard this, they were cut to the heart and said to Peter and to the other apostles, "Brothers, what should we do?" Peter said to them, "Repent, and be baptized every one of you in the name of Jesus Christ so that your sins may be forgiven; and you will receive the gift of the Holy Spirit. For the promise is for you, for your children, and for all who are far away, everyone whom the Lord our God calls to him." And he testified with many other arguments and exhorted them, saying, "Save yourselves from this corrupt generation." So those who welcomed his message were baptized, and that day about three thousand persons were added. They devoted themselves to the apostles' teaching and fellowship, to the breaking of bread and the prayers.

Chapter 4

Expanding the Church:
The Gentiles and the Mosaic Law

Acts of the Apostles 15:1–31

Who Wrote It?

Saint Luke the Evangelist wrote the Acts of the Apostles. Luke lived at the same time as many of Jesus's followers, but he was different from most of them. First, he was not one of the original disciples. Second, he was a Gentile—someone who was not a Jew. Third, he was not from Galilee or Jerusalem. He is believed to have been from Antioch, a city located about 275 miles north of Jerusalem on the Mediterranean Sea. Tradition holds that he was a doctor, and we know from his writings that he had a strong commitment to justice for those who were ill, and for all outsiders.

When Was It Written?

Most Catholic Scripture scholars believe that the Acts of the Apostles was written between AD 70 and AD 90.

Why Was It Written?

After the Holy Spirit filled the disciples and formed the Church, the believers in Jesus went out from Jerusalem to announce the message of God's salvation. During the earliest times, those who received the disciples' message and believed in Jesus were Jews. In fact, Christianity was more like a movement within Judaism than it was a separate religion. Gentiles soon heard the message as well and began to believe in salvation through Jesus Christ. This spreading of Christianity to the Gentiles actually presented a problem for the Church: how to answer the question, "Must these Gentile believers also become Jews by circumcision and by following the Mosaic Law in order to become Christians?" Some people in the Church believed that the Gentiles should become Jews; others believed otherwise. To answer the question about Gentile believers, the disciples gathered for the Council of Jerusalem.

The Council of Jerusalem gave official approval to the idea expressed in Luke's Gospel: salvation is for everybody, even for the Gentiles and other outsiders. This radical decision meant that the early Christians had to dramatically change the practice of their faith. Imagine how difficult it would be for those in power in any group or system to welcome new members who are sure to disrupt the status quo. Those who are happy with the way things are would not be pleased with many changes. Luke was trying to advance some big changes in a somewhat closed system. He told the story of the Council of Jerusalem in order to spread the word about the council's decision.

Why Is It Still Important Today?

The decision at the Council of Jerusalem was monumental. If the Church had demanded that Christian converts become Jewish, Christianity might have remained a small movement within Judaism. But the council's decision opened the way for all to receive the message of God's salvation in Jesus Christ.

Even today in the Church, we might want to keep things just as they are. But outsiders such as immigrants, juveniles who have committed crimes, and those who are poor still need to be actively welcomed into God's salvation. Luke's story is important because it reminds us that everyone is welcome.

Primary Source: Acts of the Apostles 15:1–31

Then certain individuals came down from Judea and were teaching the brothers, "Unless you are circumcised according to the custom of Moses, you cannot be saved." And after Paul and Barnabas had no small dissension and debate with them, Paul and Barnabas and some of the others were appointed to go up to Jerusalem to discuss this question with the apostles and the elders. So they were sent on their way by the church, and as they passed through both Phoenicia and Samaria, they reported the conversion of the Gentiles, and brought great joy to all the believers. When they came to Jerusalem, they were welcomed by the church and the apostles and the elders, and they reported all that God had done with them. But some believers who belonged to the sect of the Pharisees stood up and said, "It is necessary for them to be circumcised and ordered to keep the law of Moses."

The apostles and the elders met together to consider this matter. After there had been much debate, Peter stood up and said to them, "My brothers, you know that in the early days God made a choice among you, that I should be the one through whom the Gentiles would hear the message of the good news and become believers. And God, who knows the human heart, testified to them by giving them the Holy Spirit, just as he did to us; and in cleansing their hearts by faith he has made no distinction between them and us. Now therefore why are you putting God to the test by placing on the neck of the disciples a yoke that neither our ancestors nor we have been able to bear? On the contrary, we believe that we will be saved through the grace of the Lord Jesus, just as they will."

The whole assembly kept silence, and listened to Barnabas and Paul as they told of all the signs and wonders that God had done through them among the Gentiles. After they finished speaking, James replied, "My brothers, listen to me. Simeon has related how God first looked favorably on the Gentiles, to take from among them a people for his name. This agrees with the words of the prophets, as it is written,

'After this I will return,
and I will rebuild the dwelling of David,
which has fallen;
from its ruins I will rebuild it,
and I will set it up,
so that all other peoples may seek the Lord—
even all the Gentiles over whom my name has been called.
Thus says the Lord, who has been making these things
known from long ago.'

Therefore I have reached the decision that we should not trouble those Gentiles who are turning to God, but we should write to them to abstain only from things polluted by idols and from fornication and from whatever has been strangled and from blood. For in every city, for generations past, Moses has had those who proclaim him, for he has been read aloud every sabbath in the synagogues."

Then the apostles and the elders, with the consent of the whole church, decided to choose men from among their members and to send them to Antioch with Paul and Barnabas. They sent Judas called Barsabbas, and Silas, leaders among the brothers, with the following letter: "The brothers, both the apostles and the elders, to the believers of Gentile origin in Antioch and Syria and Cilicia, greetings. Since we have heard that certain persons who have gone out from us, though with no instructions from us, have said things to disturb you and have unsettled your minds, we have decided unanimously to choose representatives and send them to you, along with our beloved Barnabas and Paul, who have risked their lives for the sake of our Lord Jesus Christ. We have therefore sent Judas and Silas, who themselves will tell you the same things by word of mouth. For it has seemed good to the Holy Spirit and to us to impose on you no further burden than these essentials: that you abstain from what has been sacrificed to idols and from blood and from what is strangled and from fornication. If you keep yourselves from these, you will do well. Farewell."

So they were sent off and went down to Antioch. When they gathered the congregation together, they delivered the letter. When its members read it, they rejoiced at the exhortation.

Saint Paul's Letter to the Galatians 2:1–21

Who Wrote It?

Saint Paul wrote the Letter to the Galatians. He was among the most dynamic preachers and evangelists in the early Church. Paul founded churches throughout the land between Jerusalem and Rome and wrote nine other letters in the New Testament.

When Was It Written?

This letter was written about AD 54, twenty-five years before Saint Luke wrote the Acts of the Apostles.

Why Was It Written?

Saint Paul was writing to a community of Gentiles who had converted to Christianity under his guidance. After he left them, other missionaries came to those new Christians and caused confusion. The interlopers told the new Christians that Paul was not a true disciple and that they had to follow the Mosaic Law in order to be true converts.

Paul, who was an expert in Mosaic Law, saw the futility of this reasoning. Like Saint Luke, he knew that salvation was in Jesus, not in the Law. And as Luke would later do in his own writing, Paul cited higher authorities to back up what he said.

Why Is It Still Important Today?

Today we can still get caught up in thinking that following the rules will save us. Rules are important, but they are not the ultimate way of salvation. The Church teaches that God's salvation comes through Jesus Christ. A person who becomes a slave to the rules risks losing the heart of faith, which is a relationship with Jesus that is lived in moral and compassionate acts toward others.

That Saint Paul did not act independently is an important observation. Rather, Paul acted in union with the Church leaders in Jerusalem, setting an example that demonstrates the unity the Church still strives to reach.

Primary Source: Saint Paul's Letter to the Galations 2:1–21

Then after fourteen years I went up again to Jerusalem with Barnabas, taking Titus along with me. I went up in response to a revelation. Then I laid before them (though only in a private meeting with the acknowledged leaders) the gospel that I proclaim among the Gentiles, in order to make sure that I was not running, or had not run, in vain. But even Titus, who was with me, was not compelled to be circumcised, though he was a Greek. But because of false believers secretly brought in, who slipped in to spy on the freedom we have in Christ Jesus, so that they might enslave us—we did not submit to them even for a moment, so that the truth of the gospel might always remain with you. And from those who were supposed to be acknowledged leaders (what they actually were makes no difference to me; God shows no partiality)—those leaders contributed nothing to me. On the contrary, when they saw that I had been entrusted with the gospel for the uncircumcised, just as Peter had been entrusted with the gospel for the circumcised (for he who worked through Peter making him an apostle to the circumcised also worked through me in sending me to the Gentiles), and when James and Cephas and John, who were acknowledged pillars, recognized the grace that had been given to me, they gave to Barnabas and me the right hand of fellowship, agreeing that we should go to the Gentiles and they to the circumcised. They asked only one thing, that we remember the poor, which was actually what I was eager to do.

But when Cephas came to Antioch, I opposed him to his face, because he stood self-condemned; for until certain people came from James, he used to eat with the Gentiles. But after they came, he drew back and kept himself separate for fear of the circumcision faction. And the other Jews joined him in this hypocrisy, so that even Barnabas was led astray by their hypocrisy. But when I saw that they were not acting consistently with the truth of the gospel, I said to Cephas before them all, "If you, though a Jew, live like a Gentile and not like a Jew, how can you compel the Gentiles to live like Jews?" We ourselves are Jews by birth and not Gentile sinners; yet we know that a person is justified not by the works of the law but through faith in Jesus Christ. And we have come to believe in Christ Jesus, so that we might be justified by faith in Christ, and not by doing the works of the law, because no one will be justified by the works of the law. But if, in our effort to be justified in Christ, we ourselves have been found to be sinners, is Christ then a servant of sin? Certainly not! But if I build up again the very things that I once tore down, then I demonstrate that I am a transgressor. For through the law I died to the law, so that I might live to God. I have been crucified with Christ; and it is no longer I who live, but it is Christ who lives in me. And the life I now live in the flesh I live by faith in the Son of God, who loved me and gave himself for me. I do not nullify the grace of God; for if justification comes through the law, then Christ died for nothing.

Chapter 5

From Movement to Institution:
Practices and Guidelines for the Early Church

The Didache

Who Wrote It?

Didache (DIH-duh-kay) is the Greek word for "teaching." The *Didache,* also called *The Teaching of the Twelve Apostles,* was surely not written by the Apostles. Rather, it was probably formed by some leaders in the early Church.

When Was It Written?

The *Didache* was more compiled than written, with the final version probably assembled into a single document in the late first or early second century. But some sections, especially the beginning, might have been originally written in AD 45, a mere fifteen years after Jesus's Resurrection. Despite its age, the *Didache* is a relatively new document for the Church because a full version of the original text was not discovered until the nineteenth century.

Why Was It Written?

The *Didache* was written to provide the many Christian communities with a uniform set of practices. The New Testament is filled with examples of zealous missionaries giving conflicting messages to new converts and leading them astray. The growing Church saw a need to set down

have lot of passion about spreading the word of christ

some regulations to maintain unity. The writing of the *Didache* represents a shift away from an apparent movement Church toward a more structured and institutional Church led by the Holy Spirit.

Why Is It Still Important Today?

Many of the reforms of the Second Vatican Council, especially in liturgy and in Church structure, are based on the teachings of the Church found in the *Didache* and other early works. Understanding the central teachings of these early documents is key to fully comprehending the historical and spiritual tradition of the modern Church. First, the *Didache* provides a kind of minicatechesis, emphasizing the essential teachings that all new Christians should know. Second, it offers instructions on fasting, ritual, initiation, prayer, and Eucharistic communion. It also includes what may be the earliest known example of a Eucharistic prayer. Third, the *Didache* treats the Church's organization, including the roles of bishops and deacons. Finally, it deals with the future of the Church and its ultimate glorification when the Lord returns on the last day.

Primary Source: *The Didache*

The Law of Perfection and Foods

See "that no one leads you astray" from this way of the teaching, since such a one's teaching is godless.

If you can bear the Lord's full yoke, you will be perfect. But if you cannot, then do you what can.

Now about food: undertake what you can. But keep strictly away from what is offered to idols, for that implies worshiping dead gods.

Preparation for Baptism and Its Modes

Now about baptism: this is how to baptize. Give public instruction on all these points, and then "baptize" in running water, "in the name of the Father and of the Son and of the Holy Spirit." If you do not have running water, baptize in some other. If you cannot in cold, then in warm. If you have neither, then pour water on the head three times "in the name of the Father, Son, and Holy Spirit." Before the baptism, moreover, the one who baptizes and the one being baptized must fast, and any others who can. And you must tell the one being baptized to fast for one or two days beforehand.

Fasts and Prayers

Your fasts must not be identical with those of the hypocrites. They fast on Mondays and Thursdays; but you should fast on Wednesdays and Fridays.

You must not pray like the hypocrites, but "pray as follows" as the Lord bid us in his gospel:

"Our Father in heaven, hallowed be your name; your Kingdom come; your will be done on earth as it is in heaven; give us today our bread for the morrow; and forgive us our debts as we forgive our debtors. And do not lead us into temptation, but save us from the evil one, for yours is the power and the glory forever."

You should pray in this way three times a day.

Eucharist, Church, and Kingdom of God

Now about the Eucharist: This is how to give thanks: First in connection with the cup:

"We thank you, our Father, for the holy vine of David, your child, which you have revealed through Jesus, your child. To you be glory forever."

Then in connection with the piece [broken off the loaf]:

"We thank you, our Father, for the life and knowledge which you have revealed through Jesus, your child. To you be glory forever.

"As this piece [of bread] was scattered over the hills and then was brought together and made one, so let your Church be brought together from the ends of the earth into your Kingdom. For yours is the glory and the power through Jesus Christ forever."

The Lord's Prayer

The *Didache* includes a version of the Lord's Prayer that is very close to the version in the Gospel of Matthew. However, the *Didache* version might be the first recorded instance of the addition of the doxology, which we pray as "for the kingdom, the power, and the glory are yours, now and for ever." For centuries Catholics did not include the doxology when praying the Lord's Prayer, although other faith traditions did. In the reform of the liturgy after the Second Vatican Council, the doxology was added to the Lord's Prayer prayed at Mass.

You must not let anyone eat or drink of your Eucharist except those baptized in the Lord's name. For in reference to this the Lord said, "Do not give what is sacred to dogs."

After you have finished your meal, say grace in this way:

"We thank you, holy Father, for your sacred name which you have lodged in our hearts, and for the knowledge and faith and immortality which you have revealed through Jesus, your child. To you be glory forever.

"Almighty Master, 'you have created everything' for the sake of your name, and have given men food and drink to enjoy that they may thank you. But to us you have given spiritual food and drink and eternal life through Jesus, your child.

"Above all, we thank you that you are mighty. To you be glory forever.

"Remember, Lord, your Church, to save it from all evil and to make it perfect by your love. Make it holy, 'and gather' it 'together from the four winds' into your Kingdom which you have made ready for it. For yours is the power and the glory forever."

"Let Grace come and let this world pass away."

"Hosanna to the God of David!"

"If anyone is holy, let him come. If not, let him repent."

"Our Lord, come!"

"Amen."

In the case of prophets, however, you should let them give thanks in their own way.

Worship on the Lord's Day

On every Lord's Day—his special day—come together and break bread and give thanks; first confessing your sins so that your sacrifice may be pure. Anyone at variance with his neighbor must not join you, until they are reconciled, lest your sacrifice be defiled. For it was of this sacrifice that the Lord said, "Always and everywhere offer me a pure sacrifice; for I am a great King, says the Lord, and my name is marveled at by the nations."

The Unity of Bishop and Deacons

You must, then, elect for yourselves bishops and deacons who are a credit to the Lord, men who are gentle, generous, faithful, and well tried. For their ministry to you is identical with that of the prophets and teachers. You must not, therefore, despise them, for along with the prophets and teachers they enjoy a place of honor among you.

Furthermore, do not reprove each other angrily, but quietly, as you find it in the gospel. Moreover, if anyone has wronged his neighbor, nobody must speak to him, and he must not hear a word from you, until he repents. Say your prayers, give your charity, and do everything just as you find it in the gospel of our Lord.

Eschatology: Last Things and the Great Day of Christ's Coming

study of end-times

"Watch" over your life: do not let "your lamps" go out, and do not keep "your loins ungirded"; but "be ready," for "you do not know the hour when our Lord is coming." Meet together frequently in your search for what is good for your souls, since "a lifetime of faith will be of no advantage" to you unless you prove perfect at the very last. For in the final days multitudes of false prophets and seducers will appear. Sheep will turn into wolves, and love into hatred. For with the increase of iniquity men will hate, persecute, and betray each other. And then the world deceiver will appear in the guise of God's Son. He will work "signs and wonders" and the earth will fall into his hands and he will commit outrages such as have never occurred before. Then mankind will come to the fiery trial "and many will fall away" and perish, "but those who persevere" in their faith "will be saved" by the Curse himself. Then "there will appear the signs" of the Truth: first the sign of stretched-out [hands] in heaven; then the sign of "a trumpet's blast," and thirdly the resurrection of the dead, though not of all the dead, but as it has been said: "The Lord will come and all his saints with him. Then the world will see the Lord coming on the clouds of the sky."

Election

The reference in the *Didache* to electing bishops and deacons does not necessarily mean an election in which people vote for their favorite candidate. The election referred to is more a sense of God's choosing (electing) a candidate, a choice that becomes evident through a process of discernment within the community.

Chapter 6

Executions and Torture: Treatment of Christians During Roman Persecution

Pliny's Questions to Emperor Trajan Concerning Policy Toward Christians

Who Wrote It?

Pliny the Younger wrote his letter to Emperor Trajan when he was governor of Bithynia (now Turkey), then part of the Roman Empire. Pliny governed the region from AD 100 until his death in AD 113.

When Was It Written?

The letter was written in AD 112.

Why Was It Written?

Pliny wrote this letter to the Roman emperor Trajan to seek his advice on the treatment of Christians. Despite the fact that the Christians posed no real threat to him or to the Roman Empire, Pliny decided to execute arrested Christians if they refused to worship the Roman gods and deny their faith in Jesus. As a relatively new governor, he was not sure whether his actions were legal. Therefore, he turned to Trajan.

机 ！ 撒 我是毛

Why Is It Still Important Today?

Pliny's letter is the first known document that indicates how the Roman government acted toward Christians after Christianity separated from Judaism. For both Rome and the Church, the legal system's taking Christianity so seriously was a new practice. Jesus's ordeal before Pilate is often considered the first Christian trial. But for the Roman Empire, Jesus represented the Jewish faith, not Christianity. Likewise, Christians had been persecuted before Pliny's letter, but Romans had viewed Christianity as a Jewish sect until that time. Pliny set a new precedent by treating Christianity as a crime, thus setting the stage for the persecutions that would take place in the second and third centuries.

This important document reveals the great sacrifice suffered by the ancestors in the Christian faith. Moreover, the document offers strength to those who still suffer because they are Christians, whether they are high school students who stand firm in their morals or imprisoned Christians in a foreign land. The example of the early martyrs inspires Christians to live the Gospel in the face of opposition.

Primary Source: Pliny's Questions to Emperor Trajan Concerning Policy Toward Christians

It is my custom, my Lord, to refer to you all things concerning which I am in doubt. For who can better guide my indecision or enlighten my ignorance?

I have never taken part in the trials of Christians: hence I do not know for what crime nor to what extent it is customary to punish or investigate. I have been in no little doubt as to whether any discrimination is made for age, or whether the treatment of the weakest does not differ from that of the stronger; whether pardon is granted in case of repentance, or whether he who has ever been a Christian gains nothing by having ceased to be one; whether the *name* itself without the proof of crimes, or the crimes, inseparably connected with the *name*, are punished. Meanwhile, I have followed this procedure in the case of those who have been brought before me as Christians. I asked them whether they were Christians a second and a third time and with threats of punishment; I questioned those who confessed; I ordered those who were obstinate to be executed. For I did not doubt that, whatever it was that they confessed, their stubbornness and inflexible obstinacy ought certainly to be punished. There were others of similar madness, who because they were Roman citizens, I have noted for sending to the City. Soon, the crime spreading, as is usual when attention is called to it, more cases arose.

Anonymous Accusation

Roman spies were a serious threat to the Christian community. These spies posed as people interested in becoming Christians. Once they made their way into the community, the spies would turn in the names of the Christians to the Roman government. This spying activity was one reason why the early Church adopted the practice of having sponsors for people interested in becoming Christians. If a person wanted to enter the Church, a member of the community had to sponsor him or her. The sponsor would vouch for the person's sincerity and for his or her conversion to the Christian way of life. After years of scrutiny, the convert would enter the Church either at the Easter Vigil or during Pentecost.

An anonymous accusation containing many names was presented. Those who denied that they were or had been Christians, ought, I thought, to be dismissed since they repeated after me a prayer to the gods and made supplication with incense and wine to your image, which I had ordered to be brought for the purpose together with the statues of the gods, and since besides they cursed Christ, not one of which things they say, those who are really Christians can be compelled to do. Others, accused by the informer, said that they were Christians and afterwards denied it; in fact they had been but had ceased to be, some many years ago, some even twenty years before. All both worshipped your image and the statues of the gods, and cursed Christ. They continued to maintain that this was the amount of their fault or error, that on a fixed day they were accustomed to come together before daylight and to sing by turns a hymn to Christ as a god, and that they bound themselves by oath, not for some crime but that they would not commit robbery, theft, or adultery, that they would not betray a trust nor deny a deposit when called upon. After this it was their custom to disperse and to come together again to partake of food, of an ordinary and harmless kind, however; even this they had ceased to do after the publication of my edict in which according to your command I had forbidden associations. Hence I believed it the more necessary to examine two female slaves, who were called deaconesses, in order to find out what was true, and to do it by torture. I found nothing but a vicious, extravagant superstition. Consequently I have postponed the examination and make haste to consult you. For it seemed to me that the subject would justify consultation, especially on account of the number of those in peril. For many of all ages, of every rank, and even of both sexes are and will be called into danger. The infection of this superstition has not only spread to the cities but even to the villages and country districts. It seems possible to stay it and bring about a reform. It is plain enough that the temples, which had been almost deserted, have begun to be frequented again, that the sacred rites, which had been neglected for a long time, have begun to be restored, and that fodder for victims, for which till now there was scarcely a purchaser, is sold. From which one may readily judge what a number of men can be reclaimed if repentance is permitted.

Deaconesses

Deaconesses were women who had important roles in the early Church. Bishop, priest, and deacon are ministries in the Church to which men are ordained. Although history does not indicate that deaconesses were ordained, the role of these women and their significance in the life of the Christian community is evident. They led women in prayer; they served the community's widows; and they assisted in the Baptism of women.

"Emperor Trajan's Reply to Pliny's Questions"

Who Wrote It?

Trajan, the emperor of Rome from AD 98 to AD 117, wrote the reply to Pliny.

When Was It Written?

Trajan responded to governor Pliny's letter in AD 112.

Why Was It Written?

Trajan responded to Pliny's request for guidance. He assured Pliny that the governor had been acting according to the law. But he also cautioned Pliny not to seek out Christians and not to accept anonymous charges.

Secundus

Secundus is the Latin word for "second." In this context, secundus is a title for a second-tier official such as a governor.

Why Is It Still Important Today?

Pliny was merely a governor. Trajan held the real power. If Trajan, as the emperor of Rome, had reprimanded Pliny for executing Christians, he might have set a precedent for a more tolerant attitude on the part of the empire toward Christianity. Instead, Trajan affirmed Pliny's actions, thereby giving the official seal of approval for persecuting and executing Christians.

Even so, the persecutions under Trajan were not continuous and widespread. Although some famous martyrs, such as Saint Ignatius of Antioch, died during this time, Trajan's response to Pliny allowed Christians to practice their religion as long as such activities didn't disturb anyone.

Trajan's response remains important because it challenges us to think about the way Christians should live. Will they keep quiet about their faith to stay out of trouble? Or will they live "out loud," giving the world a clear message about Jesus Christ?

Primary Source: Emperor Trajan's Reply to Pliny's Questions

You have followed the correct procedure, my Secundus, in conducting the cases of those who were accused before you as Christians, for no general rule can be laid down as a set form. They ought not to be sought out; if they are brought before you and convicted they ought to be punished; provided that he who denies that he is a Christian, and proves this by making supplication to our gods, however much he may have been under suspicion in the past, shall secure pardon on repentance. In the case of no crime should attention be paid to anonymous charges, for they afford a bad precedent and are not worthy of our age.

Chapter 7

The Blood of the Martyrs:
A Witness to Love for Jesus

The Martyrdom of Saints Perpetua and Felicitas

Who Wrote It?

This selection primarily consists of Saint Perpetua's diary. When she wrote her diary, she was in her early twenties and newly married, with a baby who was still nursing. Her parents were still alive, and she had all the things one hoped for as a young adult. But as a new convert to Christianity, she was on fire for her faith. Because of this zeal for Jesus Christ, Perpetua was martyred in the North African city of Carthage in 202 or 203. In addition to the selections from Perpetua's diary selections, this chapter includes an introduction and a conclusion written by an unknown editor.

When Was It Written?

Saint Perpetua wrote the diary entries from prison in 202 or 203. It is unclear when the final editor added her or his introduction and conclusion.

Why Was It Written?

Saint Perpetua wrote her prison diary as an account of her persecution and as a testament to her faith in Jesus Christ. As a young adult with a new family and living parents, Perpetua had a lot to live for. We know, and she knew, that she could have been accepted back into the Church, even if she had publicly rejected Christ. In those times of persecution, denying one's faith to escape death and then seeking forgiveness was somewhat common. Even Saint Peter rejected Christ and was forgiven. But her first love was Jesus Christ, and for his sake she was willing to accept anything. Both her diary and her life stand as witness to her first love. With such a new and passionate love for Jesus, Perpetua insisted that she be martyred, even when she had several opportunities to escape death.

Why Is It Still Important Today?

Saint Perpetua's story is difficult to read today. We might find that we want her to make another choice. We might find that we want her to save herself, especially for the sake of her baby and her family. But Perpetua's story, then and now, is an example of heroic faith. This story is told and retold to give courage to those who have less resolve. If they were faced with the same conditions, most Christians would find it difficult to make the same choice that Perpetua made. Nevertheless, we all face difficult choices. Perpetua's story gives us strength to choose to do the right thing, regardless of the consequences.

Primary Source:
The Martyrdom of Saints Perpetua and Felicitas

A number of young catechumens were arrested, Revocatus and his fellow slave Felicitas, Saturninus and Secundulus, and with them Vibia Perpetua, a newly married woman of good family and upbringing. Her mother and father were still alive and one of her two brothers was a catechumen like herself. She was about twenty-two years old and had an infant son at the breast. (Now from this point on the entire account of her ordeal is her own, according to her own ideas and in the way that she herself wrote it down.)

While we were still under arrest (she said) my father out of love for me was trying to persuade me and shake my resolution. "Father," said I, "do you see this vase here, for example, or waterport or whatever?"

"Yes, I do," said he.

And I told him: "Could it be called by any other name than what it is?"

And he said: "No."

"Well, so too I cannot be called anything other than what I am, a Christian."

At this my father was so angered by the word "Christian" that he moved towards me as though he would pluck my eyes out. But he left it at that and departed, vanquished along with his diabolical arguments.

For a few days afterwards I gave thanks to the Lord that I was separated from my father, and I was comforted by his absence. During these few days I was baptized, and I was inspired by the Spirit not to ask for any other favor after the water but simply the perseverance of the flesh. A few days later we were lodged in the prison; and I was terrified, as I had never before been in such a dark hole. . . .

One day while we were eating breakfast we were suddenly hurried off for a hearing. We arrived at the forum, and straight away the story went about the neighborhood near the forum and a huge crowd gathered. We walked up to the prisoner's dock. All the others when questioned admitted their guilt. Then, when it came my turn, my father appeared with my son, dragged me from the step, and said: "Perform the sacrifice—have pity on your baby!"

Hilarianus the governor, who had received his judicial powers as the successor of the late proconsul Minucius Timinianus, said to me: "Have pity on your father's grey head; have pity on your infant son. Offer the sacrifice for the welfare of the emperors."

"I will not," I retorted.

"Are you a Christian?" said Hilarianus.

And I said: "Yes, I am."

When my father persisted in trying to dissuade me, Hilarianus ordered him to be thrown to the ground and beaten with a rod. I felt sorry for father, just as if I myself had been beaten. I felt sorry for his pathetic old age.

Then Hilarianus passed sentence on all of us: we were condemned to the beasts, and we returned to prison in high spirits. . . .

Perform the Sacrifice

Saint Perpetua was being asked to make a sacrifice to the Roman god(s).

Condemned to the Beasts

Being "condemned to the beast" meant that the condemned person would be placed in an arena to fend for himself or herself as hungry wild animals were released.

Some days later, an adjutant named Pudens, who was in charge of the prison, began to show us great honour, realizing that we possessed some great power within us. And he began to allow many visitors to see us for our mutual comfort.

Now the day of the contest was approaching, and my father came to see me overwhelmed with sorrow. He started tearing the hairs from his beard and threw them on the ground; he then threw himself on the ground and began to curse his old age and to say such words as would move all creation. I felt sorry for his unhappy old age.

The day before we were to fight with the beasts I saw the following vision. Pomponius the deacon came to the prison gates and began to knock violently. I went out and opened the gate for him. He was dressed in an unbelted white tunic, wearing elaborate sandals. And he said to me: "Perpetua, come; we are waiting for you."

Then he took my hand and we began to walk through rough and broken country. At last we came to the amphitheatre out of breath, and he led me into the centre of the arena.

Then he told me: "Do not be afraid. I am here, struggling with you." Then he left. . . .

The day of their victory dawned, and they marched from the prison to the amphitheatre joyfully as though they were going to heaven, with calm faces, trembling, if at all, with joy rather than fear. Perpetua went along with shining countenance and calm step, as the beloved of God, as a wife of Christ, putting down everyone's stare by her own intense gaze. With them also was Felicitas, glad that she had safely given birth so that now she could fight the beasts, going from one blood bath to another, from the midwife to the gladiator, ready to wash after childbirth in a second baptism. *→ her own blood*

They were then led up to the gates and the men were forced to put on the robes of priests of Saturn, the women the dress of the priestesses of Ceres. But the noble Perpetua strenuously resisted this to the end. *don't mock us*

"We came to this of our own free will, that our freedom should not be violated. We agreed to pledge our lives provided that we would do no such thing. You agreed with us to do this."

Even injustice recognized justice. The military tribune agreed. They were to be brought into the arena just as they were. Perpetua then began to sing a psalm: she was already treading on the head of the

Egyptian. Revocatus, Saturninus, and Saturus began to warn the on-looking mob. Then when they came within sight of Hilarianus, they suggested by their motions and gestures: "You have condemned us, but God will condemn you" was what they were saying.

At this the crowds became enraged and demanded that they be scourged before a line of gladiators. And they rejoiced at this that they had obtained a share in the Lord's sufferings.

But he who said, *"Ask and you shall receive,"* answered their prayer by giving each one the death he had asked for. For whenever they would discuss among themselves their desire for martyrdom, Saturninus indeed insisted that he wanted to be exposed to all the different beasts, that his crown might be all the more glorious. And so at the outset of the contest he and Revocatus were matched with a leopard, and then while in the stocks they were attacked by a bear. As for Saturus, he dreaded nothing more than a bear, and he counted on being killed by one bite of a leopard. Then he was matched with a wild boar; but the gladiator who had tied him to the animal was gored by the boar and died a few days after the contest, whereas Saturus was only dragged along. Then when he was bound in the stocks awaiting the bear, the animal refused to come out of the cages, so that Saturus was called back once more unhurt.

For the young women, however, the Devil had prepared a mad heifer. This was an unusual animal, but it was chosen that their sex might be matched with that of the beast. So they were stripped naked, placed in nets and thus brought out into the arena. Even the crowd was horrified when they saw that one was a delicate young girl and the other was a woman fresh from childbirth with the milk still dripping from her breasts. And so they were brought back again and dressed in unbelted tunics.

First the heifer tossed Perpetua and she fell on her back. Then sitting up she pulled down the tunic that was ripped along the side so that it covered her thighs, thinking more of her modesty than of her pain. Next she asked for a pin to fasten her untidy hair: for it was not right that a martyr should die with her hair in disorder, lest she might seem to be mourning in her hour of triumph.

Then she got up. And seeing that Felicitas had been crushed to the ground, she went over to her, gave her hand, and lifted her up. Then the two stood side by side. But the cruelty of the mob was by now appeased, and so they were called back through the Gate of Life.

There Perpetua was held up by a man named Rusticus who was at the time a catechumen and kept close to her. She awoke from a kind of sleep (so absorbed had she been in ecstasy in the Spirit) and she began to look about her. Then to the amazement of all she said: "When are we going to be thrown to that heifer or whatever it is?"

When told that this had already happened, she refused to believe it until she noticed the marks of her rough experience on her person and her dress. Then she called for her brother and spoke to him together with the catechumens and said: "You must all stand fast in the faith and love one another, and do not be weakened by what we have gone through."

At another gate Saturus was earnestly addressing the soldier Pudens. "It is exactly", he said, "as I foretold and predicted. So far not one animal has touched me. So now you may believe me with all your heart: I am going in there and I shall be finished off with one bite of the leopard." And immediately as the contest was coming to a close a leopard was let loose, and after one bite Saturus was so drenched with blood that as he came away the mob roared in witness to his second baptism: "Well washed! Well washed!" For well washed indeed was one who had been bathed in this manner.

Then he said to the soldier Pudens: "Good-bye. Remember me, and remember the faith. These things should not disturb you but rather strengthen you."

And with this he asked Pudens for a ring from his finger, and dipping it into his wound he gave it back to him again as a pledge and as a record of his bloodshed.

Shortly after he [Saturus] was thrown unconscious with the rest in the usual spot to have his throat cut. But the mob asked that their bodies be brought out into the open that their eyes might be the guilty witnesses of the sword that pierced their flesh. And so the martyrs got up and went to the spot of their own accord as the people wanted them to, and kissing one another they sealed their martyrdom with the ritual kiss of peace. The others took the sword in silence and without moving, especially Saturus, who being the first to climb the stairway was the first to die. For once again he was waiting for Perpetua. Perpetua, however, had yet to taste more pain. She screamed as she was struck on the bone; then she took the trembling hand of the young gladiator and guided it to her throat. It was as though so great a woman, feared as she was by the unclean spirit, <u>could not be dispatched unless she</u> <u>herself were willing</u>.

Ah, most valiant and blessed martyrs! Truly are you called and chosen for the glory of Christ Jesus our Lord! And any man who exalts, honours, and worships his glory should read for the consolation of the Church these new deeds of heroism which are no less significant than the tales of old. For these new manifestations of virtue will bear witness to one and the same Spirit who still operates, and to God the Father almighty, to his Son Jesus Christ our Lord, to whom is splendour and immeasurable power for all the ages. Amen.

N₁- Narrator 1
P -

Chapter 8

New Freedom: The Roman Empire Offers Toleration to Christians

Edict of Toleration

Who Wrote It?

The Roman Emperor Galerius wrote the Edict of Toleration. He became emperor after a distinguished career in the military where he led the Roman army to many victories in the eastern part of the empire. In 293, Emperor Diocletian (284–305) appointed him to serve as Caesar of the eastern part of the Roman Empire. Afflicted by a terrible illness in 305, Diocletian resigned as emperor, opening the way for Galerius to rule the empire.

Diocletian had implemented the fiercest persecution of Christians by the Romans. However, historians believe Diocletian persecuted the Christians at the urging of Galerius, who believed that Christianity was a grave threat to the unity of the Roman Empire. He thought that if the empire were to survive, Christianity had to be wiped out.

When Was It Written?

The Edict of Toleration was written in 311.

Why Was It Written?

Galerius continued the persecution of the Christians that began under Diocletian. The new emperor believed that uniform religious practices would help ensure the unity of the empire; therefore, Christians were forced to offer sacrifices to the Roman gods. In the face of such fierce persecution, many Christians did indeed abandon worship of Jesus. But they also abandoned worship of any god. They did not want to commit the sin of apostasy, the sin of worshipping a false god. Committing such a sin meant excommunication, or removal and separation from the Church. When faced with such consequences, Christians preferred not to worship at all rather than commit such a deadly sin.

In 311, Galerius contracted a horrible disease. The affliction left him with open sores on his body that smelled so bad that doctors refused to treat him. He urgently requested prayers—all prayers, any prayers. However, he realized that a large group of people was not praying for him because he had forced them to stop worshipping. This large group consisted of the former Christians. He issued the Edict of Toleration, which allowed the Christians to pray to their god, the God of Jesus Christ, and allowed them to worship in private.

Why Is It Still Important Today?

The Edict of Toleration is often overshadowed by the Edict of Milan that followed. But the Edict of Toleration demonstrated that the tide was turning against the devastating persecution the Christians suffered. It serves today as a sign of hope for those who suffer religious persecution worldwide.

Primary Source: Edict of Toleration

Among other arrangements which we are always accustomed to make for the prosperity and welfare of the republic, we had desired formerly to bring all things into harmony with the ancient laws and public order of the Romans, and to provide that even the Christians who had left the religion of their fathers should come back to reason; since, indeed, the Christians themselves, for some reason, had followed such a caprice and had fallen into such a folly that they would not obey the institutes of antiquity, which perchance their own ancestors

Institutes of Antiquity

Institutes of antiquity were the ancient religious practices of the Roman Empire. They included the worship of gods such as Mars and Apollo.

had first established; but at their own will and pleasure, they would thus make laws unto themselves which they should observe and would collect various peoples in diverse places in congregations. Finally when our law had been promulgated to the effect that they should conform to the institutes of antiquity, many were subdued by the fear of danger, many even suffered death. And yet since most of them persevered in their determination, and we saw that they neither paid the reverence and awe due to the gods nor worshipped the God of the Christians, in view of our most mild clemency and the constant habit by which we are accustomed to grant indulgence to all, we thought that we ought to grant our most prompt indulgence also to these, so that they may again be Christians and may hold their conventicles, provided they do nothing contrary to good order. But we shall tell the magistrates in another letter what they ought to do.

Wherefore, for this our indulgence, they ought to pray to their God for our safety, for that of the republic, and for their own, that the republic may continue uninjured on every side, and that they may be able to live securely in their homes.

This edict is published at Nicomedia on the day before the Kalends of May, in our eighth consulship and the second of Maximinus.

Edict of Milan

Who Wrote It?

The Edict of Milan states that Constantine Augustus and Licinius Augustus issued the monumental edict. It would be hard to overstate the importance of the Emperor Constantine in the history of Christianity. He granted complete tolerance to Christianity in the Roman Empire, and he convened the first ecumenical council, the Council of Nicaea. As the ruler in the eastern part of the empire, Licinius Augustus issued the edict as well to signify that the entire empire would tolerate Christianity.

Ecumenical Council

An ecumenical council is the gathering of bishops and theologians from around the world for the purpose of defining Catholic doctrine or of voicing the Church's position on or approach to a particular matter.

When Was It Written?

The Edict of Milan was written in 313.

Why Was It Written?

Many stories about the conversion of Constantine have circulated. Some say he converted for political reasons. Others say he converted because he had a vision of Christ before a battle. Others say he converted because his mother, Helena, was a Christian. We may never know the reason for his conversion, but we know he converted to Christianity and granted greater freedom to Christians. The Edict of Toleration allowed Christians to pray outside of the public eye. The Edict of Milan returned the land and the worship spaces to Christians that had been seized during the persecution. Although the Edict of Milan did not make Christianity the official religion of the empire, it gave Christianity equal status with the Roman pagan religions.

Why Is It Still Important Today?

The Edict of Milan is arguably the single most important document in Christian history. The case has been made that it took the power out of Christianity. This line of thought says that Christianity can be authentic only under persecution. Others argue that Christians were finally free to evangelize and bring everyone into the Church. Both arguments arise from a desire for Christians to fully live their faith and witness to the Good News of Jesus Christ.

Primary Source: Edict of Milan

When I, Constantine Augustus, as well as I Licinius Augustus fortunately met near Mediolanurn (Milan), and were considering everything that pertained to the public welfare and security, we thought, among other things which we saw would be for the good of many, those regulations pertaining to the reverence of the Divinity ought certainly to be made first, so that we might grant to the Christians and others full authority to observe that religion which each preferred; whence any Divinity whatsoever in the seat of the heavens may be propitious and kindly disposed to us and all who are placed under our rule. And thus by this wholesome counsel and most upright provision we thought to arrange that no one whatsoever should be denied the opportunity to give his heart to the observance of the Christian religion, of that religion which he should think best for himself, so that the Supreme Deity, to whose worship we freely yield our hearts, may show in all things His usual favor and benevolence. Therefore, your Worship should know that it has pleased us to remove all conditions whatsoever, which were in the rescripts formerly given to you officially, concerning the Christians and now any one of these who wishes to observe Christian religion may do so freely and openly, without molestation. We thought it fit to commend these things most fully to your care that you may know that we have given to those Christians free and unrestricted opportunity of religious worship. When you see that this has been granted to them by us, your Worship will know that we have also conceded to other religions the right of open and free observance of their worship for the sake of the peace of our times, that each one may have the free opportunity to worship as he pleases; this regulation is made we that we may not seem to detract from any dignity or any religion.

Moreover, in the case of the Christians especially we esteemed it best to order that if it happens anyone heretofore has bought from our treasury from anyone whatsoever, those places where they were previously accustomed to assemble, concerning which a certain decree had been made and a letter sent to you officially, the same shall be restored to the Christians without payment or any claim of recompense and without any kind of fraud or deception. Those, moreover, who have obtained the same by gift, are likewise to return them at once to the Christians. Besides, both those who have purchased and those who have secured them by gift, are to appeal to the vicar if they seek any recompense from our bounty, that they may be cared for through our clemency. All this property ought to be delivered at once to the community of the Christians through your intercession, and without delay. And since these Christians are known to have possessed not only those places in which they were accustomed to assemble, but also other property, namely the churches, belonging to them as a corporation and not as individuals, all these things which we have included under the above law, you will order to be restored, without any hesitation or controversy at all, to these Christians, that is to say to the corporations and their conventicles: providing, of course, that the above arrangements be followed so that those who return the same without payment, as we have said, may hope for an indemnity from our bounty. In all these circumstances you ought to tender your most efficacious intervention to the community of the Christians, that our command may be carried into effect as quickly as possible, whereby, moreover, through our clemency, public order may be secured. Let this be done so that, as we have said above, Divine favor towards us, which, under the most important circumstances we have already experienced, may, for all time, preserve and prosper our successes together with the good of the state. Moreover, in order that the statement of this decree of our good will may come to the notice of all, this rescript, published by your decree, shall be announced everywhere and brought to the knowledge of all, so that the decree of this, our benevolence, cannot be concealed.

Chapter 9.

Two Cities:
The Earthly and the Heavenly

The City of God

Who Wrote It?

Saint Augustine was born in 354 and died in 430. He was a bishop in the North African city of Hippo. His ability to express the richness of the Christian faith in both the spoken and the written word has earned him the title "Doctor of the Church." He spent his earlier life in sinful living. But after his conversion in 386, he devoted his life to the Lord's service. He became a priest in 391 and the bishop of Hippo in 396. He was, and remains, one of the most important of all theologians.

Doctor of the Church

A doctor of the Church is one whose teaching has had such influence that she or he has become an especially important figure in Christian history. To date, only thirty-three people have been given the title.

Why Was It Written?

In the early 400s, tribes from northern Europe invaded Rome and took control of the city. Many people claimed the Roman gods were angry and allowed the destruction of the city as punishment for the conversion of the empire to Christianity. To counter those accusations, Saint Augustine wrote *The City of God* to defend the empire's conversion.

He began by describing the terrible things that happened in the world long before Christianity existed. Then he told how the events of his time and the events of the future were to be interpreted through the eyes of Christian faith.

When Was It Written?

The writing of *The City of God* spanned several years. Saint Augustine began writing it in 413 and concluded the work in 426.

Why Is It Still Important Today?

Saint Augustine's defense of Christianity is an outline of salvation history. Augustine showed how all of history led up to history's culminating event: the life, death, and Resurrection of Jesus Christ. In detailing the world's events, Augustine made it clear that the fullness of God's plan cannot be fully known by us but is revealed to us as God wills, with the clearest revelation found in the sacred Scriptures. Augustine said that we cannot and should not try to explain history without reference to the sacred Scriptures.

During Augustine's time, not everyone shared his concern to keep their spirituality based in God's Word. Some attempted to explain history through the fortunes and the misfortunes of the Roman (Christian) Empire. Others tried to find in current events the signs of Christ's immediate return in glory. People today also try to do the same things. But reading Augustine closely and heeding his caution to keep the Word of God reminds Christians that no one can fully know God's plan; rather, it is revealed gradually over time.

Primary Source: *The City of God*

Book XIV, Chapter 28

Accordingly, two cities have been formed by two loves: the earthly by the love of self, even to the contempt of God; the heavenly by the love of God, even to the contempt of self. The former, in a word, glories in itself, the latter in the Lord. For the one seeks glory from men; but the greatest glory of the other is God, the witness of conscience. The one lifts up its head in its own glory; the other says to its

God, "Thou art my glory, and the lifter up of mine head." In the one, the princes and the nations it subdues are ruled by the love of ruling; in the other, the princes and the subjects serve one another in love, the latter obeying, while the former take thought for all. The one delights in its own strength, represented in the persons of its rulers; the other says to its God, "I will love Thee, O Lord, my strength." And therefore the wise men of the one city, living according to man, have sought for profit to their own bodies or souls, or both, and those who have known God "glorified Him not as God, neither were thankful, but became vain in their imaginations, and their foolish heart was darkened; professing themselves to be wise,"—that is, glorying in their own wisdom, and being possessed by pride—"they became fools, and changed the glory of the incorruptible God into an image made like to corruptible man, and to birds, and four-footed beasts, and creeping things." For they were either leaders or followers of the people in adoring images, "and worshipped and served the creature more than the Creator, who is blessed for ever." But in the other city there is no human wisdom, but only godliness, which offers due worship to the true God, and looks for its reward in the society of the saints, of holy angels as well as holy men, "that God may be all in all."

Book XV, Chapter 4

But the earthly city, which shall not be everlasting (for it will no longer be a city when it has been committed to the extreme penalty), has its good in this world, and rejoices in it with such joy as such things can afford. But as this is not a good which can discharge its devotees of all distresses, this city is often divided against itself by litigations, wars, quarrels, and such victories as are either life-destroying or short-lived. For each part of it that arms against another part of it seeks to triumph over the nations through itself in bondage to vice. If, when it has conquered, it is inflated with pride, its victory is life-destroying; but if it turns its thoughts upon the common casualties of our mortal condition, and is rather anxious concerning the disasters that may befall it than elated with the successes already achieved, this victory, though of a higher kind, is still only short-lived; for it cannot abidingly rule over those whom it has victoriously subjugated. But the things which this city desires cannot justly be said to be evil, for it is itself, in its own kind, better than all other human good. For it desires earthly peace for the sake of enjoying earthly goods, and it makes war in order to attain to this peace; since, if it has conquered, and there remains no one to resist it, it enjoys a peace which it had not while there were opposing parties who contested for the enjoyment of those things which were too small to satisfy both. This peace is purchased by toilsome wars; it is obtained by what they style a glorious victory. Now, when victory remains with the party which had the juster cause, who hesitates to congratulate the victor, and style it a desirable peace? These things, then, are good things, and without doubt the gifts of God. But if they neglect the better things of the heavenly city, which are secured by eternal victory and peace never-ending, and so inordinately covet these present good things that they believe them to be the only desirable things, or love them better than those things which are believed to be better—if this be so, then it is necessary that misery follow and ever increase.

Divided Against Itself

Many people misunderstand the idea of the two cities. Those who misunderstand the comparison think that heaven is good and the earth is bad. In this chapter, Saint Augustine says that the earthly city is good but divided against itself. On the earth, battles rage between war and peace, injustice and justice, sin and holiness. In the heavenly city, these conflicts will be resolved.

Selections from Book XXII, Chapter 30

How great shall be that felicity, which shall be tainted with no evil, which shall lack no good, and which shall afford leisure for the praises of God, who shall be all in all! For I know not what other employment there can be where no lassitude shall slacken activity, nor any want stimulate to labor. . . .

But who can conceive, not to say describe, what degrees of honor and glory shall be awarded to the various degrees of merit? Yet it cannot be doubted that there shall be degrees. And in that blessed city there shall be this great blessing, that no inferior shall envy any superior, as now the archangels are not envied by the angels, because no one will wish to be what he has not received, though bound in strictest concord with him who has received; as in the body the finger does not seek to be the eye, though both members are harmoniously included in the complete structure of the body. And thus, along with his gift, greater or less, each shall receive this further gift of contentment to desire no more than he has. . . .

This Sabbath shall appear still more clearly if we count the ages as days, in accordance with the periods of time defined in Scripture, for that period will be found to be the seventh. The first age, as the first day, extends from Adam to the deluge; the second from the deluge to Abraham, equalling the first, not in length of time, but in the number of generations, there being ten in each. From Abraham to the advent of Christ there are, as the evangelist Matthew calculates, three periods, in each of which are fourteen generations—one period from Abraham to David, a second from David to the captivity, a third from the captivity to the birth of Christ in the flesh. There are thus five ages in all. The sixth is now passing, and cannot be measured by any number of generations, as it has been said, "It is not for you to know the times, which the Father hath put in His own power." After this period God shall rest as on the seventh day, when He shall give us (who shall be the seventh day) rest in Himself. But there is not now space to treat of these ages; suffice it to say that the seventh shall be our Sabbath, which shall be brought to a close, not by an evening, but by the Lord's day, as an eighth and eternal day, consecrated by the resurrection of Christ, and

Degrees of Merit

The enjoyment of heaven can be described like a musical performance. Two people may be at a concert, but one person enjoys the concert more than the other because she has prepared herself better. She knows the story of the musicians. She has learned all there is to know about the music. She anticipates her favorite parts. Two people are at the same event, but one is enjoying it more. Saint Augustine says that through a life of holiness, one will be better prepared to enjoy the awesome experience of heaven.

prefiguring the eternal repose not only of the spirit, but also of the body. There we shall rest and see, see and love, love and praise. This is what shall be in the end without end. For what other end do we propose to ourselves than to attain to the kingdom of which there is no end?

I think I have now, by God's help, discharged my obligation in writing this large work. Let those who think I have said too little, or those who think I have said too much, forgive me; and let those who think I have said just enough give thanks, not to me, but rather join me in giving thanks to God. Amen.

The Eighth Day

The idea of the "Eighth Day" was important to the Christians—it was a symbol of heaven. God created the world in seven days, and then on the eighth day, he made a new and eternal creation. The Eighth Day refers to the Resurrection of Jesus. All who share in Jesus's Resurrection share in the Eighth Day. For this reason, many ancient baptismal fonts are eight-sided.

Chapter 10

True God Became True Human: Statements on Who Jesus Is

"Definition of the Faith"

Who Wrote It?

The bishops gathered for the Council of Chalcedon wrote "Definition of the Faith." However, this statement was based, in part, on a letter written by Pope Saint Leo the Great in 449.

When Was It Written?

In 451, bishops from throughout the Christian world gathered at the city of Chalcedon, a location on the outskirts of modern-day Istanbul, Turkey, for an ecumenical council. "The Definition of Faith" was written at this council.

Why Was It Written?

"Definition of Faith" was written to settle a controversy over the relationship between the divinity of Christ and the humanity of Christ. The Nicaea Council, held in the year 325, answered the question of Jesus's divinity. That council said that Jesus was truly and fully God. But if Christ is truly and fully God, how can he be human, too? The answer is not simple. In fact, one of the greatest thinkers of the early Church, Saint Gregory of Nyssa, said he didn't know the answer.

But one person, Nestorius, thought he knew the answer. He taught that Christ had two separate, different natures. Nestorius made such a sharp distinction, for example, that he concluded only Christ's human nature suffered on the cross and his divine nature did not. But another group of thinkers said Jesus had only one nature—a nature that was a mixture of human and divine.

In response to those two different ways of thinking about Jesus being both God and human, the Council of Chalcedon put forth a carefully worded

statement saying that Christ, indeed, had two natures—truly God and truly human. The statement also said these natures were fully joined in one person, meaning that whatever was experienced by one nature (for example, suffering on the cross) was also experienced by the other.

Why Is It Still Important Today?

The "Definition of the Faith" is not a mere collection of words that have no bearing on the lives of everyday men and women. Rather, this statement on Jesus's nature is absolutely necessary for understanding what salvation is. Christians now and throughout the centuries face the great questions of life, mental suffering, and even death with courage and hope because of their faith in Jesus. Knowing that Jesus is fully human, just like they are, gives them hope. During Jesus's earthly life, he felt the same fear, the same pain, the same anguish, the same doubt as they do. But Jesus's ability to feel pain and suffering was not enough to offer real hope for salvation. The fact that Jesus is also a savior, the divine Son of God, completes the hope for salvation. The Catholic prayer for salvation can be found in a sentence the priest says at Mass: "May we come to share in the divinity of Christ, who humbled himself to share in our humanity." Somehow, if Jesus is like us in our humanity, then we can be one with him in his divinity. This is the mystery of salvation. Without the "Definition of the Faith," the Church would have no words to express this mystery.

Primary Source: "Definition of the Faith"

The holy and great and ecumenical synod, gathered in virtue of God's grace and at the command of our pious and Christ-loving emperors, the Augusti Marcian and Valentinian, in Chalcedon, metropolis of the eparchy of Bithynia, in the martyry of the holy and triumphant martyr Euphemia, has laid down the following decrees.

Our Lord and Savior Jesus Christ, as he was establishing his disciples in understanding of the faith, stated, "My peace I leave with you, my peace I give to you" [John 14:27], in order that no one should speak differently from his neighbor about the teachings of true religion, but that, on the contrary, the proclamation of the faith should be exhibited as the same for all.

Since the evil one does not cease using his tares to plant over the seeds of true religion and is always discovering something against the truth, the Lord, for this reason, with his customary providential care for the human race, raised this most pious and faithful emperor to zeal and convoked the leaders of the priesthood from every quarter to himself, so that as the grace of Christ, the Lord of us all, was working, every defilement of falsehood might be removed from Christ's sheep and she might be enriched by the plantings of truth.

And this we have done. By unanimous vote we have driven away the teachings of error, and we have renewed the inerrant faith of the Fathers. We have proclaimed to all the Symbol of the Three Hundred and Eighteen and we have endorsed, as belonging to the same family, the Fathers who accepted that covenant of true religion—we mean the one hundred and eighty who subsequently assembled in the great city of Constantinople and themselves validated the same faith.

We therefore decree (keeping to the ranking and to all the decisions about the faith established by the holy synod which met at Ephesus under the leadership of Celestine of Rome and Cyril of

Alexandria, of blessed memory) that primary authority shall belong to the exposition of the correct and blameless faith composed by the three hundred and eighteen holy and blessed fathers who gathered in Nicaea when Constantine, of devout memory, was emperor; and that authority shall belong to the decrees which derive from the one hundred and eighty holy fathers in Constantinople, which they laid down for the destruction of the heresies which had grown up at that time and for the corroboration of our same catholic and apostolic faith.

The Symbol of the 318 at Nicaea

"We believe in one God, Father, Ruler of all, the maker of heaven and earth and of all things seen and unseen.

"And in one Lord Jesus Christ, the only-begotten Son of God, begotten from the Father before all ages, true God from true God, begotten not made, of one essence with the Father; through whom all things were made; who for us human beings and for our salvation came down and was incarnate and became human; and suffered, and rose on the third day and went up into the heavens and is seated at the right hand of the Father, and is coming to judge the living and the dead.

"And in the Holy Spirit.

"But those who say, 'There was a "when" when he was not' and 'Before he was begotten he did not exist' and 'He came into existence out of nothing,' or who say that the Son of God is 'from another hypostasis or essence,' or 'mutable' or 'alterable'—them the catholic and apostolic church anathematizes."

Council of Nicaea

Emperor Constantine convened an ecumenical council in the city of Nicaea in 325. He wanted to settle a debate about Jesus's divinity. Everyone agreed that Jesus was the *Word* (in Greek *Logos*) made flesh. But the dispute was over whether the Logos was a creation of the Father or was equal to the Father. The Council of Nicaea wrote the Nicene Creed, which is recited at Mass on Sunday, to answer this question. The Creed says that the Logos is equal to the Father. He is fully God and eternal just like the Father is eternal.

Anathema

Anathema is the Church's strongest condemnation. It literally means to be cursed.

The Symbol of the 180 at Constantinople

"We believe in one God, Father, Ruler of all, Maker of heaven and earth and of all things visible and invisible.

Council of Constantinople

In 381, the Roman Emperor Theodosius convened an ecumenical council at Constantinople to answer lingering questions about the Trinity. Tradition holds that 180 bishops gathered for that council.

"And in one Lord Jesus Christ, the only-begotten Son of God, begotten from the Father before all ages, Light from Light, true God from true God, begotten not made, of one essence with the Father, through whom all things were made; who for us human beings and for our salvation came down from heaven and was incarnate from the Holy Spirit and Mary the Virgin and became human; and was crucified for us under Pontius Pilate, and suffered, and was buried, and rose on the third day in accordance with the Scriptures; and went up into the heavens, and is seated at the right hand of the Father, and is coming again with glory to judge the living and the dead. His Kingdom will have no end.

"And in the Holy Spirit, the Lord, the Lifegiver, who proceeds from the Father, who is worshiped and glorified together with the Father and the Son, who spoke through the prophets: in one holy catholic and apostolic church. We confess one baptism for the remission of sins. We expect the resurrection of the dead and the life of the coming world."

This wise and saving symbol of the divine grace should have been sufficient for the knowledge and support of true religion, for it gives the complete teaching about the Father and the Son and the Holy Spirit, and to those who receive it faithfully it interprets the Lord's becoming human. Nevertheless, since those who attempt to set aside the proclamation of the truth have given birth to empty talk through their own heresies (some daring to corrupt the mystery of the Lord's dispensation on our behalf and deny the title "Mother of God" to the Virgin, others introducing a confusion and mixture, and stupidly imagining that there is one nature of the flesh and the deity, and suggesting impossibly that in virtue of this confusion the divine nature of the Only Begotten is passible): for this reason, this holy, great, and ecumenical synod now assembled, seeking to deprive them of every device against the truth, and teaching the ever-unchanging character of the proclamation, has decreed in the first place that the Creed of the Three Hundred and Eighteen holy fathers shall stand untouched. Furthermore, because of those who take up arms against the Holy Spirit, it confirms the teaching about the essence of the Spirit which was later handed down by the one hundred and eighty holy fathers gathered in the imperial city. They made this teaching known to everyone, not by adding anything which was left out by their predecessors but by clarifying, through scriptural testimonies, their understanding of the Holy Spirit in opposition to those who were trying to reject his rule.

Nestorius

Nestorius had two beliefs that the Church condemned. First, he believed that Jesus did not have a human soul. He thought the Logos took the place of a human soul in Jesus. But the Church said that if Jesus had been truly human, he must have had a human soul. Second, he didn't think Mary should be called the Mother of God. But the Church said that if Jesus was truly God and equal to the Father, then "Mother of God" is a correct title for Mary.

And because of those who attempt to corrupt the mystery of the dispensation, shamelessly pretending that the one born of the holy Mary was an ordinary human being, it has received, as in agreement [with this faith], the synodical letters of the blessed Cyril, then shepherd of the Alexandrian church, to Nestorius and the Orientals, for the sake of refuting the follies of Nestorius and for the instruction of those who, in religious zeal, seek understanding of the saving Symbol.

With these letters, for the confirmation of the orthodox teachings, it has appropriately included the letter which the most blessed and holy archbishop Leo, who presides in the great and elder Rome, wrote to the holy archbishop Flavian for the removal of the error of Eutyches, for it agrees with the confession of the great Peter and is a common pillar against those who think wrongly.

For [this synod] sets itself against those who attempt to split up the mystery of the dispensation into a duality of sons; and those who dare to assert that the deity of the Only Begotten is passible it expels from the college of priests; and it opposes those who conceive of a confusion or mixture in the case of the two natures of Christ; and it drives out those who foolishly think that the "form of a slave" which was assumed by him from among us is of a heavenly, or some other, essence; and it anathematizes those who make up the teaching that before the union there are two natures of the Lord, but imagine that after the union there is one.

Following, therefore, the holy fathers, we confess one and the same Son, who is our Lord Jesus Christ, and we all agree in teaching that this very same Son is complete in his deity and complete—the very same—in his humanity, truly God and truly a human being, this very same one being composed of a rational soul and a body, coessential with the Father as to his deity and coessential with us—the very same one—as to his humanity, being like us in every respect apart from sin. As to his deity, he was born from the Father before the ages, but as to his humanity, the very same one was born in the last days from the Virgin Mary, the Mother of God, for our sake and the sake of our salvation: one and the same Christ, Son, Lord, Only Begotten, acknowledged to be unconfusedly, unalterably, undividedly, inseparably in two natures, since the difference of the natures is not destroyed because of the union, but on the contrary, the character of each nature is preserved and comes together in one person and one hypostasis, not divided or torn into two persons but one and the same Son and only-begotten God, Logos, Lord Jesus Christ—just as in earlier times the prophets and also the Lord Jesus Christ himself taught us about him, and the symbol of our Fathers transmitted to us.

Since, therefore, these matters have been determined by us with all possible precision and care, the holy and ecumenical synod decrees that it is not permissible for anyone to propose, write, compose, think, teach anything else. But those who dare to compose another creed or to bring forward or teach or transmit another symbol to people who want to turn to the knowledge of truth from Hellenism or Judaism or from any heresy whatever—such persons, if they are bishops or clergy, are deposed, the bishops from their episcopate and the clergy from their office; but if they are monks or laity they are anathematized.

Chapter 11

Missionary Pope: Saint Gregory the Great Brings the Light of Christ to England

Ecclesiastical History of the English People

Who Wrote It?

Saint Bede the Venerable was a Church historian and a doctor of the Church. He is believed to have been born in 672, and he died in 735. Bede spent his life as a priest and monk at a monastery in England. Throughout his time in the monastery, he loved to study the Scriptures and to interpret them for the other monks. His writings certainly indicate that he loved the life of the monastery.

When Was It Written?

Saint Bede began writing the *Ecclesiastical History of the English People* in 731, near the end of his life.

Why Was It Written?

Saint Bede's history was commissioned by King Ceolwulph. Although someone else commissioned the work, Bede also had a message he wanted to communicate. He wanted to establish the

Doctor of the Church

A doctor of the Church is one whose teaching has had such influence that she or he has become an especially important figure in Christian history. To date, only thirty-three people have been given the title.

legitimacy and authority of a Rome-centered Christianity as opposed to the Celtic Christianity of the Irish monks. For this reason, he expounded upon the ways England benefited from the missionary work of the great Roman Pope and fellow doctor of the Church, Saint Gregory the Great.

Why Is It Still Important Today?

Saint Bede's account is the first written history of the Roman Catholic Church in England. Today this history is still the primary source for much of what is known about that time in England. Even though it is a history book, its author, it should be remembered, was Bede, who was first of all a monk. More than just writing down facts and dates, he tried to show how God continues to act through history. In particular, he wanted to show how God acts through the Pope and the Roman Catholic Church to guide Christians throughout all time into God's truth. Through such teaching and guidance, humanity's greatest hungers can be satisfied.

Primary Source: *Ecclesiastical History of the English People*

In the year of our Lord 605, having ruled the apostolic Roman Church most illustriously for thirteen years, six months, and ten days, the blessed Pope Gregory died and was taken up to his eternal home in heaven. And it is fitting that he should receive special mention in this history, since it was through his zeal that our English nation was brought from the bondage of Satan to the Faith of Christ, and we may rightly term him our own apostle. For during his pontificate, while he exercised supreme authority over all the churches of Christendom that had already long since been converted, he transformed our still idolatrous nation into a church of Christ. So we may rightly describe him as our own apostle, for while others may not regard him in this light, he was certainly an apostle to our own nation, and we are the seal of his apostleship in the Lord.

Gregory was Roman-born, son of Gordian, and came of a noble and devout family. Felix, once bishop of the same apostolic see, a man of high distinction in the Church of Christ, was one of his ancestors, and Gregory maintained this family tradition by the nobility and devotion of his religious life. By God's grace, he employed his recognized worldly position solely to win the glory of eternal honour, for he soon retired from secular life and sought admission to a monastery. . . .

Gregory also wrote a notable book, *The Pastoral Office*, in which he describes in clear terms the qualities essential in those who rule the Church, showing how they should live; how they should carefully instruct all their people; and how they should always bear in mind their own frailty. . . . Further, he compiled a book of answers in reply to the questions of Saint Augustine, first bishop of the English nation. . . . He also wrote a large number of personal letters. The extent of his writings is a source of amazement when one considers that throughout his youth he was often in agony from gastric pain, and frequently troubled by a slow fever. But in all these afflictions he reflected that holy scripture says: "The Lord scourgeth every son that He receiveth," and the greater his worldly sufferings, the greater his assurance of eternal joy.

Much might be said of his imperishable genius, which was unimpaired even by the most severe physical afflictions; for while other popes devoted themselves to building churches and enriching them with costly ornaments, Gregory's sole concern was to save souls. He regularly gave whatever money he had to relieve the poor, in order that "his righteousness might remain for ever, and his horn be exalted with honour." . . . In addition to his deeds of kindness and justice, we should remember with gratitude how Gregory saved our nation from the grasp of the ancient

Question of Celibacy for Priests

Saint Bede the Venerable mentions a person named Felix in his letter. He says that Felix was both a bishop and an ancestor of Saint Gregory the Great. This may raise the question, How can a bishop have descendants?

The practice of celibacy enjoys a long tradition in the Church. Even during the time when the New Testament was being written, evidence suggests, some people lived celibately. While that tradition grew through the centuries, celibacy was not a rule for being a priest or a bishop in the Roman Catholic Church until the eleventh century. At that time, another Pope Gregory—Pope Gregory VII—made priestly celibacy a part of his sweeping reform of the Church.

Apostolic See

After the Holy Spirit came at Pentecost, Jesus's Apostles spread out across the known world to found Christian communities. Once they established the communities, the Apostles appointed bishops to lead those fledgling communities in their absence. Those bishops taught and led with the same authority the Apostles had. Likewise, the next generation of bishops taught and led with the same authority the Apostles had. This line of succession has continued for generation after generation of bishops. Because of this direct line of succession from the Apostles, a bishop's ministry is described as "apostolic."

The word *see* comes from the Latin word that means "seat" or "chair." See refers to the place where authoritative decisions are made. The pope's line of authority comes from Saint Peter, the Apostles' leader; therefore, the pope's apostolic see is also referred to as "the chair of Saint Peter."

Enemy by the preachers whom he sent us, and brought it into the abiding liberty of God. He was full of joy at its conversion and salvation, as he mentions in his Commentary on Job: "The Britons, who formerly knew only their own barbaric tongue, have long since begun to cry the Hebrew Alleluia to the praise of God. The once restless sea now lies quiet before the feet of His saints, and its ungovernable rages, which no earthly princes could tame by the sword, are now quelled at the simple word of His priests in the fear of God. Heathen nations who never trembled before armed hosts now accept and obey the teachings of the humble. For now that the grace of the knowledge of God has enlightened them and they see His heavenly truths and mighty wonders, the fear of God restrains them from their former wickedness, and they desire with all their hearts to win the prize of eternal life." . . .

Among many other matters, blessed Pope Gregory decreed that Mass should be said over the tombs of the holy Apostles Peter and Paul in their churches. He also introduced into the Canon of the Mass three excellent and valuable petitions: Order our days in Thy peace, preserve us from eternal damnation, and number us in the flock of Thine elect, Through Christ our Lord. . . .

I must here relate a story which shows Gregory's deep desire for the salvation of our nation. We are told that one day some merchants who had recently arrived in Rome displayed their many wares in the crowded market-place. Among other merchandise Gregory saw some boys exposed for sale. These had fair complexions, fine-cut features, and fair hair. Looking at them with interest, he enquired what country and race they came from. "They come from Britain," he was told, "where all the people have this appearance." He then asked whether the people were Christians, or whether they were still ignorant heathens. "They are pagans," he was informed. "Alas!" said Gregory with a heartfelt sigh: "how sad that such handsome folk are still in the grasp of the Author of darkness, and that faces of such beauty conceal minds ignorant of God's grace! What is the name of this race?" "They are called Angles," he was told. "That is appropriate," he said, "for they have angelic faces, and it is right that they should become fellow-heirs with the angels in heaven." . . .

Approaching the Pope of the apostolic Roman See for he was not yet Pope himself Gregory begged him to send preachers of the word to the English people in Britain to convert them to Christ, and declared his own eagerness to attempt the task should the Pope see fit to direct it. But this permission was not forthcoming, for although the Pope himself was willing, the citizens of Rome would not allow Gregory to go so far away from the city. But directly Gregory succeeded to the Papacy himself, he put in hand this long cherished project and sent other missionaries in his place, assisting their work by

The Pastoral Office

The Pastoral Office, also known as The Book of Pastoral Rule, describes the life a bishop should lead. The book describes how a bishop should minister to the people and also how he should be a spiritual man. The Pastoral Office was a groundbreaking book that offers insights for today's ministers.

Gregorian Masses

Saint Gregory the Great also began the practice of celebrating thirty Masses for thirty days for the salvation of someone who had died. Such Masses offered for those who have died have become known as Gregorian Masses.

his own prayers and encouragement. And I have thought it fitting to include this traditional story in the history of our Church.

"Letter to Abbot Mellitus"

Who Wrote It?

Pope Saint Gregory the Great wrote the letter to Abbot Mellitus.

When Was It Written?

Pope Saint Gregory the Great wrote the letter in 601.

Why Was It Written?

Pope Saint Gregory the Great sent Abbot Mellitus to assist Archbishop Augustine—who would later become Saint Augustine of Canterbury—in the conversion of England. The Pope wrote to offer his advice regarding the conversion of the English people.

Why Is It Still Important Today?

Reading this letter helps us better understand the role of the English Christians in the history of the Church. By the time Saint Augustine of Canterbury and his fellow missionaries went to England, all of the civilized world—that is, the Roman Empire—was a Christian society. When England became Christian, it also gained more status in the political world of the empire. It became both a secular and spiritual force to be reckoned with in the world.

From this letter, we also learn a method of evangelization that was re-emphasized at the Second Vatican Council; that is, the Catholic Church should always seek to adapt the worthy elements of any culture into Catholic practices. Adapting such practices points to the fact that the grace of God is found in all Creation.

Primary Source: "Letter to Abbot Mellitus"

Tell Augustine that he should by no means destroy the temples of the gods but rather the idols within those temples. Let him, after he has purified them with holy water, place altars and relics of the saints in them. For, if those temples are well built, they should be converted from the worship of demons to the service of the true God. Thus, seeing that their places of worship are not destroyed, the people will banish error from their hearts and come to places familiar and dear to them in acknowledgement and worship of the true God.

Further, since it has been their custom to slaughter oxen in sacrifice, they should receive some solemnity in exchange. Let them therefore, on the day of the dedication of their churches, or on the feast of the martyrs whose relics are preserved in them, build themselves huts around their one-time temples and celebrate the occasion with religious feasting. They will sacrifice and eat the animals not any more as an offering to the devil, but for the glory of God to whom, as the giver of all things, they will give thanks for having been satiated. Thus, if they are not deprived of all exterior joys, they will more easily taste the interior ones. For surely it is impossible to efface all at once everything from their strong minds, just as, when one wishes to reach the top of a mountain, he must climb by stages and step by step, not by leaps and bounds. . . .

Mention this to our brother the bishop, that he may dispose of the matter as he sees fit according to the conditions of time and place.

Chapter 12

A Father's Wisdom:
A Guide for Living in a Community

The Prologue to *The Rule of St. Benedict*

Who Wrote It?

As its title indicates, *The Rule of St. Benedict* is believed to have been written by Saint Benedict of Nursia, Italy, founder of the monastery of Monte Cassino. However, not enough evidence exists to be certain that he was indeed the author. It is known that, prior to his founding of the monastery, Benedict had been formed as a monk in the tradition of the early Egyptian monks who practiced a severe and isolated form of monasticism.

When Was It Written?

The Rule of St. Benedict was written between 530 and 560. But the author based some of the work on earlier writings that may date back to the fourth century.

Why Was It Written?

When Saint Benedict founded his own monasteries, he wanted his *Rule* to provide a middle way between the severe practices of the Egyptian monks and a life of ease. According to that middle way, the monks still had to fast, pray, and live in poverty, but they also had enough to eat and drink as well as time for prayer and recreation. Benedict sought a balance between work and prayer, and he emphasized the value of community over individual isolation.

The original monks of the fourth century fled to the desert because of the perceived negative influences of secular society. Benedict faced similar pressures. Society's stability was at risk as the old Roman Empire weakened. As a young monk, Benedict had been to the desert, but he found that living in the desert was not the answer to the secular society's negative influences. Instead, he sought to provide a monastic way of life that was fully integrated with society and yet stood apart as a source and model of hospitality, stability, and moderation. The prologue—the introduction to *The Rule of St. Benedict*—urges the monks to fervently seek the Lord as they make their way along a new path for being a monk.

> ### *Hospitality*
>
> If there is one attribute that characterizes Benedictines, it is their hospitality. While much of *The Rule of St. Benedict* has been adapted for modern times, all Benedictines take this exhortation from chapter 53 seriously: "All guests to the monastery should be welcomed as Christ, because He will say, 'I was a stranger, and you took me in'" (Matthew 25:35).

Why Is It Still Important Today?

As we enter a new millennium, fresh pressures threaten to destabilize our society and the Catholic faith. Some might advocate for Christians to isolate themselves from the greed, materialism, and self-centeredness that seems to be the driving force of so much anguish in the world. Saint Benedict might encourage today's Christians to look for God's grace in all of Creation and seek to call forth the best in everyone. The principles in *The Rule of St. Benedict* can serve as a guide for us as we seek to establish a twenty-first-century version of the middle way.

Benedict did not write his *Rule* for the superheroes of the faith. He wrote for ordinary Christians. As a result, thousands and thousands of Christians—both monks and laypeople—follow some version of the *Rule* today. The *Rule* is based on the way of Christ handed down to us in the sacred Scriptures and in sacred Tradition. It is a spiritual guide for any Christian to follow Saint Benedict's middle way.

Primary Source: The Prologue to *The Rule of St. Benedict*

Listen, my son, and with your heart hear the principles of your Master. Readily accept and faithfully follow the advice of a loving Father, so that through the labor of obedience you may return to Him from whom you have withdrawn because of the laziness of disobedience. My words are meant for you, whoever you are, who laying aside your own will, take up the all-powerful and righteous arms of obedience to fight under the true King, the Lord Jesus Christ.

First, with fervent prayer, beg of Him to finish the good work begun, so that He who has so generously considered us among His true children, may never be saddened by our evil deeds. We must serve Him always with our God-given talents so that He may not disinherit His children like an angered father, nor enraged by our sins, give us up to eternal punishment like a dreaded Lord whose worthless servants refuse to follow Him to glory.

Therefore, let us arise without delay, the Scriptures stirring us: "It is now the hour for us to awake from sleep" (Rom. 13:11). Let us open our eyes to the Divine light and attentively hear the Divine voice, calling and exhorting us daily: "Today if you shall hear his voice, harden not your hearts" (Ps. 95:7–8); and again, "He who has ears, let him hear/what the Spirit says to the Churches" (Rev. 2:7). And what does He say? "Come, you children, and listen to Me: I will teach you the fear of the Lord" (Ps. 34:11). "Run where you have the light, lest the shadows of death come upon you" (Jn. 12:35).

The Lord looks for His workman among the masses of men. He calls to him: "Who is the man that will have life, and desires to see good days?" (Ps. 34:12). And if, hearing this, you answer, "I am he," God says to you, "If you desire true and everlasting life keep your tongue from evil and make sure your lips speak without guile; renounce evil and do good; seek peace and pursue it" (Ps. 34:13–14). "If you do this, My eyes will see you, and My ears will hear your prayers" (Ps. 34:17). "And before you can call out to Me, I will say to you: 'Behold, I am here'" (Is. 58:9). What can be more pleasing, dear brothers, than the voice of the Lord's invitation? See how He shows us the way of life in His benevolence.

Let us encompass ourselves with faith and the practice of good works, and guided by the Gospel, tread the path He has cleared for us. Thus may we deserve to see Him, who has called us into His Kingdom.

If we wish to be sheltered in this Kingdom, it can be reached only through our good conduct. But let us ask our Lord (with the prophet): "Lord, who shall live in Your Kingdom? or who shall rest on Your holy mountain?" (Ps. 15:1). Once we have asked this, listen to the Lord's response as He shows us the way to His Kingdom: "He who walks without blemish and works justice, he who speaks truth in his heart, who has not been deceitful in his speech, he who has not harmed his neighbor, nor censured him, shall dwell with me" (Ps. 15:2–3). He who casts out from the innermost thoughts of his heart the Devil's suggestions for straying from God's path, making them null and void, he who takes his nascent thoughts and dashes them against Christ, as against a rock, shall dwell with Me, as shall they who, fearing the Lord, do not pride themselves on their good conduct. Rather they praise the work of the Lord (knowing that what is good in them is God-given) thus: "Not to us, O Lord, not to us, but to Your Name give glory" (Ps. 115:1). The Apostle Paul attributed nothing of his preaching to himself. "By the grace of God I am what I am" (1 Cor. 15:10). "He who glories, let him glory in the Lord" (2 Cor. 10:17). For the same reason the Lord says in the Gospel: "He who hears these my words and performs them shall be likened to a wise man who built his house upon a rock; the floods came, the winds blew and struck against the house, and it did not fall, for it was built upon a rock" (Matt. 7:24–25).

After the Lord has ended His exhortation, He waits every day for us to respond to His sacred counsels.

So that we may change from our evil ways our lives are lengthened, as in an amnesty. For the Apostle says: "Do you not know that the patience of God will lead you to repentance?" (Rom. 2:4). And "I do not will the death of the sinner, but rather that he be converted and live" (Ezek. 33:11).

We have questioned the Lord, brothers, and have heard of the conditions for living in His Kingdom; but we shall live there only if we fulfill these conditions. Therefore we must prepare ourselves, in body and soul, to fight under the commandments of holy obedience. And that which is less possible to us in nature, let us ask of God—to command the aid of His grace to help us. If, escaping the tortures of Hell, we wish to find eternal life, we must live what God wills in our lifetime, while we have the ability and chance.

The Benedictine Way of Life

Benedictines make three promises, or vows, when they become monks. They promise stability, which means they will always live in community with the abbey they join. They promise to always follow the monastic way of life. And they promise obedience to the abbot or prioress.

We are about to open a school for God's service, in which we hope nothing harsh or oppressive will be directed. For preserving charity or correcting faults, it may be necessary at times, by reason of justice, to be slightly more severe. Do not fear this and retreat, for the path to salvation is long and the entrance is narrow.

As our lives and faith progress, the heart expands and with the sweetness of love we move down the paths of God's commandments. Never departing from His guidance, remaining in the monastery until death, we patiently share in Christ's passion, so we may eventually enter into the Kingdom of God.

Chapter 13

Saint Boniface:
Missionary to the Germans

Letter Advising Saint Boniface on How to Convert the Heathens

Who Wrote It?

Daniel was the bishop of Winchester, England, from 705 to 744. He had many well-known and saintly friends, including Saint Bede the Venerable, Saint Aldhelm, and Saint Boniface.

When Was It Written?

Bishop Daniel wrote the letter to his friend Saint Boniface in 723, seven years after Boniface began his missionary work.

Why Was It Written?

As a trusted friend, Saint Boniface often sought Daniel's advice about his missionary labors. Daniel wrote the letter to support his friend and to provide some insight for an effective approach to evangelization. He instructed Saint Boniface to use logical arguments to overcome cultural elements not in harmony with Christian truths.

Why Is It Still Important Today?

The letter provides a different approach to evangelization than the one used by Saint Augustine of Canterbury and by Saint Gregory the Great. The tone of the letter and some of the words in the letter might cause discomfort to our modern ears. Referring to the native people as "heathens" and "barbarous" might seem demeaning. But the reader who looks beyond the tone and language will find a method of evangelization based on logical arguments. This method is in contrast to Gregory the Great's method. Pope Gregory's approach encourages missionaries to use the elements of a culture and to interpret them through Christian eyes. Both methods have value and are important in evangelization. However, the Second Vatican Council, it should be remembered, urged Catholics to proclaim the Gospel of Jesus Christ with fervor while also showing a humble respect for the culture of others. Such urging has been embraced by Pope John Paul II as he tried to harmonize the two approaches. He sought to appeal to people's sense of logic and order and also embraced new cultures and interpreted them in the light of the Gospel.

Primary Source: Letter Advising Saint Boniface on How to Convert the Heathens

To Boniface, honoured and beloved leader, Daniel, servant of the people of God.

Great is my joy, brother and colleague in the episcopate, that your good work has received its reward. Supported by your deep faith and great courage, you have embarked upon the conversion of heathens whose hearts have hitherto been stony and barren and with the Gospel as your ploughshare you have laboured tirelessly day after day to transform them into harvest-bearing fields. Well may the words of the prophet be applied to you: "A voice of one crying in the wilderness, etc."

Yet not less deserving of reward are they who give what help they can to such a good and deserving work by relieving the poverty of the labourers, so that they may pursue unhampered the task of preaching and begetting children to Christ. And so, moved by affection and good will, I am taking the liberty of making a few suggestions, in order to show you how,

Episcopate

Episcopate refers to people who are bishops.

in my opinion, you may overcome with the least possible trouble the resistance of this barbarous people.

Do not begin by arguing with them about the genealogies of their false gods. Accept their statement that they were begotten by other gods through the intercourse of male and female and then you will be able to prove that, as these gods and goddesses did not exist before, and were born like men, they must be men and not gods. When they have been forced to admit that their gods had a beginning, since they were begotten by others, they should be asked whether the world had a beginning or was always in existence. There is no doubt that before the universe was created there was no place in which these created gods could have subsisted or dwelt. And by "universe" I mean not merely heaven and earth which we see with our eyes but the whole extent of space which even the heathens can grasp in their imagination. If they maintain that the universe had no beginning, try to refute their arguments and bring forward convincing proofs; and if they persist in arguing, ask them, Who ruled it? How did the gods bring under their sway a universe that existed before them? Whence or by whom or when was the first god or goddess begotten? Do they believe that gods and goddesses still beget other gods and goddesses? If they do not, when did they cease and why? If they do, the number of gods must be infinite. In such a case, who is the most powerful among these different gods? Surely no mortal man can know. Yet man must take care not to offend this god who is more powerful than the rest. Do they think the gods should be worshipped for the sake of temporal and transitory benefits or for eternal and future reward? If for temporal benefit let them say in what respect the heathens are better off than the Christians. What do the heathen gods gain from the sacrifices if they already possess everything? Or why do the gods leave it to the whim of their subjects to decide what kind of tribute shall be paid? If they need such sacrifices, why do they not choose more suitable ones? If they do not need them, then the people are wrong in thinking that they can placate the gods with such offerings and victims. . . .

The heathens are frequently to be reminded of the supremacy of the Christian world and of the fact that they who still cling to outworn beliefs are in a very small minority. . . .

I pray for your welfare in Christ, my very dear colleague, and beg you to remember me.

Report to Pope Zacharias on the Foundation of Fulda Abbey

Who Wrote It?

Saint Boniface is believed to have been born in Crediton, England, in 680. He was a Benedictine monk who felt called to be a missionary. In 716, Boniface went to what is modern-day Germany and the Netherlands to minister among the people. He is now revered as the patron saint of those two countries.

When Was It Written?

Saint Boniface wrote the report in 751.

Why Was It Written?

Saint Boniface was a diligent missionary, who possessed an ingrained sense of Roman organization and protocol. He was a legate, or representative, of the Pope. Boniface's position required him to keep the Pope informed of the progress in his missionary work. Much of Boniface's work was difficult. He dealt with corruption, stubborn authorities, and a sometimes lawless population. Nevertheless, Boniface was successful. His establishment of an abbey in Fulda, Germany, was a particular source of happiness for him. His letter reveals that he wanted the Pope to be aware of that important development in his mission.

Why Is It Still Important Today?

As with the efforts of Saint Augustine of Canterbury in England, the evangelization work of Saint Boniface brought Germany into the political and spiritual sphere of Rome. Although Rome was declining as a political center, the city remained the spiritual center of the Western Church. Boniface's report offers some insight into his struggles as well as into his perseverance, patience, and even cheerfulness in the face of many challenges. Boniface's flair for organization and administration was instrumental in establishing lasting churches and abbeys throughout Germany and northern Europe. Like many saints, Boniface is a hero of the Church, and his life and fervor is an example of Christian discipleship.

Primary Source: Report to Pope Zacharias on the Foundation of Fulda Abbey

I beseech Your Gracious Highness with earnest prayer to receive with kindness and favour a priest of mine, Lull, and bearer of my letter. He brings certain confidential messages for your gracious hearing only, partly by word of mouth, partly in writing. He will also make certain enquiries of importance to me and bring me for the comfort of my old age your answers and fatherly advice given with all the authority of St. Peter, Prince of the Apostles. When you have heard and considered all these matters, if they meet with your approval, I shall strive with God's help to enlarge upon them, but if, as I fear, they may not altogether please you, I shall follow your apostolic precept and either crave your indulgence or do penance as is fitting.

To the most reverend and beloved lord and master to be revered in fear and honour, Zacharias, invested with the privilege of the apostolic office and raised to the dignity of the Apostolic See, Boniface, your humble and most unworthy servant, but your devoted legate in Germany, sends greetings of unfailing love.

When your predecessor once removed, Gregory II, of revered memory, consecrated me bishop, unworthy as I was, and sent me to preach the word of faith to the Germans, he bound me by oath to support by word and deed all

Apostolic Office and Apostolic See

After Pentecost, Jesus's Apostles spread out across the known world to found Christian communities. Once the communities were established, the Apostles appointed bishops to lead the fledgling communities in their absence. Those bishops taught and led with the same authority the Apostles had. Likewise, the next generation of bishops taught and led with the same authority the Apostles had. This line of succession has continued for generations. Because of this direct line of succession from the Apostles, a bishop's ministry is described as "apostolic."

The word *see* comes from the Latin word that means "seat" or "chair." The word refers to the place where authoritative decisions are made. The Pope's line of authority comes from Saint Peter, the Apostle's leader. Therefore, the Pope's Apostolic See is also referred to as "the chair of Saint Peter."

those bishops and priests who were canonically elected and of blameless life. This by divine grace I have tried to do. False priests, however, and hypocrites misleading the people, I was either to convert to the way of salvation or to reject and refrain from associating with them. This I have in part accomplished, but in part have not been able to maintain. In spirit I have kept my oath, because I have not agreed with them nor taken part in their counsels; but in the letter I could not avoid contact with them because when I went to the Frankish court on urgent ecclesiastical matters there were men there whom I would rather not have met.

The Pontiff also told me to make reports to the Apostolic See on the life and customs of the races I visited. And this I hope that I have done. But on the matter which I made known to you about the archbishops making their pleas for pallia from Rome, as the Franks promised they would, I crave the indulgence of the Apostolic See, because they are slow to carry out their promises. They are still discussing the matter and putting it off, and it is uncertain what they intend to do. But had it been left to me, the promise would have been kept. [136] There is a wooded place in the midst of a vast wilderness situated among the peoples to whom I am preaching. There I have placed a group of monks living under the rule of St. Benedict who are building a monastery. They are men of ascetic habits, who abstain from meat and wine and spirits, keeping no servants, but are content with the labour of their own hands. This place I have acquired by honourable effort through the help of pious and God-fearing men, especially of Carloman, formerly King of the Franks, and have dedicated it in honour of the Holy Saviour.

The Franks

The Franks were members of a confederacy of tribes that inhabited parts of what is modern-day Germany, France, and Belgium.

Here I propose with your kind permission to rest my aged and worn body for a little time and after my death to be buried here. The four peoples to whom we have preached the Word of God by the grace of God dwell, as all know, round about this place, and as long as I live and retain my faculties I can with your support be useful to them. It is my desire, sustained by your prayers and led by God's grace, to continue my close relations with you and to remain in your service among the German people to whom I was sent, and to follow your directions as it is written: [Ecclus iii.2] "Hear the judgment of your father, O my children, and so act that you may be saved. He that giveth glory to his father shall have length of days. In deed and word honour thy father that a blessing may come to thee from him, for a blessing of the father establisheth the houses of children."

Chapter 14

Conflicts of Faith:
Tensions Between the East and the West

Encyclical Letter to the Archiepiscopal Sees of the East

Who Wrote It?

Patriarch Photius of Constantinople, the author of the letter, was a controversial figure. In 857, he became the patriarch, or bishop, of Constantinople, which is located in what is modern-day Turkey. The controversy surrounding Photius involves the means by which he became the patriarch.

Ignatius, the patriarch before Photius, would not allow Bardas, one of the secular rulers, to receive Communion. Ignatius denied Communion to Bardas because the man had been living in incest with his daughter-in-law. Angry at Ignatius for refusing to give him Communion, Bardas sought to have the patriarch removed by the emperor. Photius was consecrated as a bishop and replaced Ignatius as the patriarch of Constantinople.

When Was It Written?

The date the letter was written is unknown; however, most historians believe it was written about 867.

Why Was It Written?

During the first several centuries of Christianity, most Christians were unified in their belief in Jesus and in their recognition of the bishop of Rome as the chief pastor of all Christians. But since the fourth century, tension had been growing between the Eastern, or Orthodox, Church and the Western, mostly Roman Catholic, Church. That tension came to a final and formal schism (SIH-zum), or split, between the Eastern and Western churches at the Council of Florence in 1472. Photius's letter details many of the beliefs and practices that caused the tension between the East and the West.

Photius wanted to make clear the Eastern positions on the issues, but he also tried to undermine the authority of the bishop of Rome. He wanted to undermine the Pope's authority because Pope Nicholas I said that Photius was not the legitimate patriarch of Constantinople. Photius tried to demonstrate in his letter that the Church in the West had wavered from true Christianity, and if the Church in the West had wavered, the authority of the Pope could then be called into question.

Why Is It Still Important Today?

Photius's letter represents the beginning of the formal rupture between the Western and Eastern churches. The final split did not occur until the fifteenth century, but Photius's letter marked the turning point. His letter defines the core differences that led to the schism and the task that still lies ahead in reconciling that split.

The most significant issues laid out in Photius's letter are those related to the Trinity. The understanding of the Trinity is at the center of the how both churches understand God, and each has a lot at stake. The Eastern Church does not recognize the phrase in the Nicene Creed stating that the Holy Spirit proceeds from the Father "and the Son," nor does it recognize the official teaching of the Church. However, at the Council of Florence in 1439, the Eastern Church agreed that the Holy Spirit proceeds from the Father and "and *through* the Son." In the *Catechism of the Catholic Church,* paragraph 248, the Church expresses the belief that this agreement can be the beginning point of reunification.

Primary Source:
Encyclical Letter to the Archiepiscopal Sees of the East

Encyclical letter to the archiepiscopal sees of the East, that is, Alexandria and the rest, in which the solutions of certain doubtful conclusions are considered, and that it is not permissible to say that the Holy Spirit proceeds from the Father and the Son, but from the Father alone.

Filioque: The Holy Spirit "proceeds from the Father and the Son . . ."

Understanding the Trinity was a major theological problem during the Great Schism between the Eastern and the Western churches. Translations vary, but the Creed adopted at the Council of Nicaea of 325 reads:

And in the Holy Spirit, the Lord, the giver of life, Who proceeds from the Father, Who together with the Father and the Son, is worshipped and glorified . . ."

But later the Roman Catholic Church added "who proceeds from the Father, *and the Son*." The Eastern Church believes the addition confuses the roles of the persons in the Trinity. The Roman Church believes the addition emphasizes Christ's divinity.

These [heresies of Arius, Macedonius, Nestorius Eutyches, and Dioscorus] although at one time very prominent, have been consigned to silence and oblivion. Bright and solid hope that there would be a time in the near future when no fresh contriver of impieties would spring up seemed encouraging, because in all things that the devil has attempted the opposite effect has turned out. . . .

Moreover, now the barbarian tribe of the Bulgarians, who were hostile and inimical to Christ, has been converted to a surprising degree of meekness and knowledge of God. Beyond all expectation they have in a body embraced the faith of Christ, departing from the worship of devils and of their ancestral gods, and rejecting the error of pagan superstition.

But what a wicked and malignant design, what an ungodly state of affairs! Here is the story: The previous assumption of good news has been turned into dejection, delight and joy are changed into sadness and tears. That people had not embraced the true religion of Christians for even two years when certain impious and ominous men (or by whatever name a Christian refers to them) emerged from the darkness (for they have risen up out of the West)—Oh, how will I go on to tell the rest?—These, as I have said, in a tribe so recently established in piety, which joined the Church just a short time ago, as lightning or an earthquake or a heavy hail—actually I should say, like a wild boar greedily leaping into the much loved and newly planted vineyard of the Lord with feet and bared teeth—on paths of dishonorable administration and corrupted doctrine, thus boldly dividing up the country for themselves, have brought ruin on the people. They have villainously devised to lead them away from the true and pure doctrine and from an unblemished Christian faith and in this way destroy them.

The first unlawful practice they have set up is fasting on Saturday. Such slight disregard for the traditional teaching usually leads to the complete abandonment of the entire doctrine.

They separated the first week of Lent from the rest and allowed them milk, cheese and other gluttonous practices during this time. From here they made the road of transgressions wider and wider and removed the people more and more from the straight and royal road.

Lenten Fast

The Eastern and the Orthodox Catholic churches abstain from dairy products as part of the Lenten fast, which also includes abstinence from meat, a tradition also followed by the Roman Catholic Church.

Manichaeism

Manichaeism, condemned as heresy, is the belief that created things are evil. Photius, therefore, believed that mandatory celibacy for the clergy was a rejection of a good creation—marriage.

They taught them to despise the priest living in lawful matrimony and by rejecting matrimony spread the seed of Manichaeism, while they themselves practiced adultery.

They did not shrink from reconfirming those who had been anointed by priests with the chrism, and presenting themselves as bishops, they declared the confirmation administered by priests to be useless and invalid. Whoever heard of such a preposterous idea as these insane men have produced, of confirming those who are already confirmed and thereby making full of the supernatural and divine mysteries of Christians. . . . They claim that bishops only have the right to confirm. But who made this law? Which apostle, which father of the Church, which synod made it? Where and when was this synod held? Who confirmed the resolution? If the priest is not allowed to confirm, then neither is he allowed to baptize or to offer sacrifice. He may as well return to the lay state. Whoever sacrifices the Body of the Lord and the Blood of Christ and by it sanctifies the already blessed members of the Church must certainly be able to sanctify with oil those already blessed. The priest baptizes . . . how then do you deprive him of bringing to perfection with its guard and seal the purification which he has really only begun? Then he would be only a priest in name. . . .

Confirmation

In the Roman Catholic Church, the bishop is the person who sacramentally confers the Holy Spirit, under most circumstances. In the Eastern Catholic Church, in the Orthodox Church, and during the Rite of Christian Initiation of Adults in the Roman Church, the priest sacramentally confers the Holy Spirit at Baptism.

They have not only introduced the committing of such outrages, but now the crown of all evils is sprung up. Besides these offences that have already been mentioned, they have attempted to adulterate the sacred and holy creed, which has been approved by the vote of all the ecumenical synods and has unconquerable strength, with spurious arguments, interpolated words, and rash exaggerations. They are preaching a novel doctrine: that the Holy Spirit proceeds not from the Father alone, but from the Son as well.

This is the impiety which those bishops of darkness (at least they call themselves bishops) have spread among the Bulgarians. There are also other unlawful practices which they have introduced. When the report of these things reached my ears it struck a mortal blow right to my heart. I felt just like a father who sees his own children torn to pieces and dragged about by ferocious animals and snakes. For our sufferings and labors and sweat laid the foundation for their regeneration and initiation. In proportion to these it is permissible to sympathize with the unbearable pain and misfortune of these perishing children. The greater the joy was over the rebirth of this people, the greater must be the affliction over their misfortune. I have deeply mourned and I am mourning yet. I will give my eyes no rest until I have lifted up the deceived and returned them to the house of the Lord.

These new forerunners of apostasy, these servants of the anti-Christ, who have deserved death a thousand times, . . . these deceivers and enemies of God, we have by the resolution of a holy synod sentenced, or rather declared, that by previous resolutions of synods and by apostolic laws, they are already condemned and are made manifest to all. People are so constituted by nature that they are more restrained by present and visible punishments than by previously inflicted ones. Thus because these men remain in their manifold errors, we consider them banished by public proclamation from the company of Christians. The sixty-fourth canon of the holy apostles, rejecting those who make it their practice to fast on Saturdays, says:

Anathema

Anathema, the Church's strongest condemnation, literally means "to be cursed."

"If any cleric is found fasting on the Lord's Day or on Saturday, except for one [Saturday], he is to be deposed; if a lay person is found doing this he is to be excommunicated. . . ."

The fourth canon of the Synod of Gangra, against those who have a horror for marriage, says, "If any priest who is married thinks that this forbids him from partaking in the offering when he officiates at the sacred liturgy, let him be anathema. . . ."

As for doing away with the first week [of Lent] and the re-anointing of those who were anointed at the time they were baptized, there is no need to speak, since these abuses have their condemnation in the canons already mentioned. . . .

But the blasphemy against the Holy Spirit, or rather against the whole Trinity, has nothing to compare with it, and if all the other false teachings were not present, this alone would be enough to bring ten thousand anathemas upon them. . . .

It is necessary that those whom you send as your representatives will uphold you and that they be dispatched with your full and free power, that, namely, which is bestowed upon you by the Holy Spirit. The reason for this is that they may be able to give an opinion and vote on the matter proposed and on any other matter which might be treated, with that liberty which befits the apostolic sees. This is especially the case since from Italy a synodal letter has reached us full of accusations against their Roman bishop. With it was a request not to allow the Italian Christians to perish in such a lamentable way on account of a cruel tyranny which overrides all ecclesiastical laws. But this is not the first complaint to reach us, for previously we have been informed of the situation by a priest who escaped from there and by some monks. Basilius, Zosimus, and Metrophanes have complained of this heavy yoke, and have called upon us with tears to avenge the tyranized Church. Just now several letters from different persons have arrived full of bitter complaints and tragic stories. According to the wishes of the senders, we have sent special copies of these to the apostolic sees together with this letter for your appraisal. We have done this so that the holy and ecumenical synod which is about to be convened in the Lord, will be seen to conform with the canons and will be confirmed by their unanimous vote, and thus a deep peace may take hold of the Church of Christ.

Chapter 15

Pope Against King:
The Battle Over Appointing Bishops

Correspondence Regarding Lay Investiture

Who Wrote It?

The correspondence in this chapter is between Pope Gregory VII and Emperor Henry IV. Each man was powerful and strong-willed. Gregory VII, also known as Hildebrand, was the Pope from 1073 until his death in 1085. Henry IV was emperor of the Roman Empire from 1084 until 1105, but he also served as the king of Germany from 1056 until 1084. Gregory entered the Papacy with clear ideas about the role and the power of the Pope. On the other hand, Henry IV, who centralized the power of the throne, ruled with power and authority. A collision between Gregory VII and Henry IV was inevitable.

When Was It Written?

The two men corresponded in 1075, two years into Pope Gregory VII's Papacy and during Henry IV's reign as king of Germany.

Why Was It Written?

Pope Gregory VII, a major reformer in Church history, had big ideas and set out to accomplish a lot. One of the most significant reforms he attempted was to give the Pope authority over the appointment of bishops. For about 300 years preceding Gregory VII's time as pope, the emperor, kings, and other secular leaders also had the power to appoint bishops, sometimes more power than the Pope had. The struggle to prevent kings and princes from "vesting" someone as bishop came to be known as the "lay investiture controversy." The controversy began with Gregory VII and lasted until 1122 when the emperor ceded sole control over appointing bishops to the Pope.

In claiming the right to appoint bishops—even those opposed by the Pope—Henry IV followed the example of his father, Henry III, who asserted that the power of the emperor is primary. But Gregory VII came to see such an attitude as a threat to the Church and, he believed, a violation of God's will. The letters of these two powerful leaders represent the struggle that came to a flash point with their reigns and continued after their reigns ended.

Why Is It Still Important Today?

The controversy over the appointment of bishops was, in a sense, a small part of a larger argument. What was really at stake, and what is still at stake today, is the line between the authority of the Church and the authority of government. It is a matter of separation between Church and State. If nothing else, these letters let the reader know that this battle is an old one. Perhaps they can provide some insights to resolving such tensions.

Primary Source: Correspondence Regarding Lay Investiture

A Letter from Pope Gregory VII to Emperor Henry IV

Gregory, bishop, servant of God's servants, to King Henry, greeting and the apostolic benediction—but with the understanding that he obeys the Apostolic See as becomes a Christian king.

Considering and weighing carefully to how strict a judge we must render an account of the stewardship committed to us by St. Peter, prince of the Apostles, we have hesitated to send you the apostolic benediction, since you are reported to be in voluntary communication with men who are under the censure of the Apostolic See and of a synod. If this is true, you yourself know that you cannot receive the favor of God nor the apostolic blessing unless you shall first put away

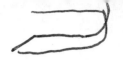

those excommunicated persons and force them to do penance and shall yourself obtain absolution and forgiveness for your sin by due repentance and satisfaction. Wherefore we counsel Your Excellency, if you feel yourself guilty in this matter, to make your confession at once to some pious bishop who, with our sanction, may impose upon you a penance suited to the offense, may absolve you and with your consent in writing may be free to send us a true report of the manner of your penance.

We marvel exceedingly that you have sent us so many devoted letters and displayed such humility by the spoken words of your legates, calling yourself a son of our Holy Mother Church and subject to us in the faith, singular in affection, a leader in devotion, commending yourself with every expression of gentleness and reverence, and yet in action showing yourself most bitterly hostile to the canons and apostolic decrees in those duties especially required by loyalty to the Church. Not to mention other cases, the way you have observed your promises in the Milan affair; made through your mother and through bishops, our colleagues, whom we sent to you, and what your intentions were in making them is evident to all. And now, heaping wounds upon wounds, you have handed over the sees of Fermo and Spoleto—if indeed a church may be given over by any human power—to persons entirely unknown to us, whereas it is not lawful to consecrate anyone except after probation and with due knowledge.

Apostolic Office and Apostolic See

After the Holy Spirit came at Pentecost, Jesus's Apostles spread out across the known world to found Christian communities. Once the communities were established, the Apostles appointed bishops to lead the fledgling communities in their absence. Those bishops taught and led with the same authority the Apostles had. Likewise, the next generation of bishops taught and led with the same authority the Apostles had. This line of succession has continued for generation after generation of bishops. Because of this direct line of succession from the Apostles, a bishop's ministry is described as "apostolic."

The word *see* comes from the Latin word that means "seat" or "chair." The word refers to the place where authoritative decisions are made. The Pope's line of authority comes from Saint Peter, the Apostle's leader. Therefore, the Pope's Apostolic See is also referred to as "the chair of Saint Peter."

It would have been becoming to you, since you confess yourself to be a son of the Church, to give more respectful attention to the master of the Church, that is, to Peter, prince of the Apostles. To him, if you are of the Lord's flock, you have been committed for your pasture, since Christ said to him: "Peter, feed my sheep [Jn 21:17]," and again: "To thee are given the keys of Heaven, and whatsoever thou shalt bind on earth shall be bound in Heaven and whatsoever thou shalt loose on earth shall be loosed in Heaven [Mt 16:19]." Now, while we, unworthy sinner that we are, stand in his place of power, still whatever you send to us, whether in writing or by word of mouth, he himself receives, and while we read what is written or hear the voice of those who speak, he discerns with subtle insight from what spirit the message comes. Wherefore Your Highness should beware lest any defect of will toward the Apostolic See be found in your words or in your messages and should pay due reverence, not to us but to Almighty God, in all matters touching the welfare of the Christian faith and the status of the Church. And this we say although our Lord deigned to declare: "He who heareth you heareth me; and he who despiseth you despiseth me" [Lk 10:16]. . . .

This edict [against lay investiture], which some who place the honor of men above that of God call an intolerable burden, we, using the right word, call rather a truth and a light necessary for salvation, and we have given judgment that it is to be heartily accepted and obeyed, not only by you and your subjects but by

Apostolic Benediction

As the person who continues the ministry of Saint Peter the Apostle, the Pope conveys a special blessing: the apostolic benediction. Because of Henry IV's disobedience, Pope Gregory VII was reluctant to give him this blessing.

Milan Affair

When Alexander II (1061–1073) was the Pope, a controversy erupted over who had appointed the legitimate bishop of Milan. A clergyman named Atto was elected bishop by supporters of the Pope, while another clergyman named Godfrey was elected by supporters of Emperor Henry IV. In that conflict, Atto became bishop of Milan and Godfrey withdrew.

all princes and peoples who confess and worship Christ—though it is our especial wish and would be especially fitting for you, that you should excel others in devotion to Christ as you are their superior in fame, in station and in valor.

Nevertheless, in order that these demands may not seem to you too burdensome or unfair we have sent you word by your own liegemen not to be troubled by this reform of an evil practice but to send us prudent and pious legates from your own people. If these can show in any reasonable way how we can moderate the decision of the holy fathers [at the Council] saving the honor of the eternal king and without peril to our own soul, we will condescend to hear their counsel. It would in fact have been the fair thing for you, even if you had not been so graciously admonished, to make reasonable inquiry of us in what respect we had offended you or assailed your honor, before you proceeded to violate the apostolic decrees. But how little you cared for our warnings or for doing right was shown by your later actions.

However, since the long-enduring patience of God summons you to improvement, we hope that with increase of understanding your heart and mind may be turned to obey the commands of God. We warn you with a father's love that you accept the rule of Christ, that you consider the peril of preferring your own honor to his, that you do not hamper by your actions the freedom of that Church which he deigned to bind to himself as a bride by a divine union, but, that she may increase as greatly as possible; you will begin to lend to Almighty God and to St. Peter, by whom also your own glory may merit increase, the aid of your valor by faithful devotion.

Now you ought to recognize your special obligation to them for the triumph over your enemies which they have granted you, and while they are making you happy and singularly prosperous, they ought to find your devotion increased by their favor to you. That the fear of God, in whose hand is all the might of kings and emperors, may impress this upon you more than any admonitions of mine, bear in mind what happened to Saul after he had won a victory by command of the prophet, how he boasted of his triumph, scorning the prophet's admonitions, and how he was rebuked by the Lord, and also what favor followed David the king as a reward for his humility in the midst of the tokens of his bravery.

sternly correct

Finally, as to what we have read in your letters and do not mention here we will give you no decided answer until your legates, Radbod, Adalbert and Odescalcus, to whom we entrust this, have returned to us and have more fully reported your decision upon the matters which we commissioned them to discuss with you.

A Letter from Emperor Henry IV to Pope Gregory VII

Henry, King not by usurpation, but by the pious ordination of God, to Hildebrand, now not Pope, but false monk:

You have deserved such a salutation as this because of the confusion you have wrought; for you left untouched no order of the Church which you could make a sharer of confusion instead of honor, of malediction instead of benediction.

For to discuss a few outstanding points among many: Not only have you dared to touch the rectors of the holy Church—the archbishops, the bishops, and the priests, anointed of the Lord as they are—but you have trodden them under foot like slaves who know not what their lord may do. In crushing them you have gained for yourself acclaim from the mouth of the rabble. You have judged that all these know nothing, while you alone know everything. In any case, you have sedulously used this knowledge not for edification, but for destruction, so greatly that we may believe Saint Gregory, whose name you have arrogated to yourself, rightly made this prophesy of you when he said: "From the abundance of his subjects, the mind of the prelate is often exalted, and he thinks that he has more knowledge than anyone else, since he sees that he has more power than anyone else."

And we, indeed, bore with all these abuses, since we were eager to preserve the honor of the Apostolic See. But you construed our humility as fear, and so you were emboldened to rise up even against the royal power itself, granted to us by God. You dared to threaten to take the kingship away from us—as though we had received the kingship from you, as though kingship and empire were in your hand and not in the hand of God.

Our Lord, Jesus Christ, has called us to kingship, but has not called you to the priesthood. For you have risen by these steps: namely, by cunning, which the monastic profession abhors, to money; by money to favor; by favor to the sword. By the sword you have come to the throne of peace, and from the throne of peace you have destroyed the peace. You have armed subjects against their prelates; you who have not been called by God have taught that our bishops who have been called by God are to be spurned; you have usurped for laymen the bishops' ministry over priests, with the result that these laymen depose and condemn the very men whom the laymen themselves received as teachers from the hand of God, through the imposition of the hands of bishops.

You have also touched me, one who, though unworthy, has been anointed to kingship among the anointed. This wrong you have done to me, although as the tradition of the holy Fathers has taught, I am to be judged by God alone and am not to be deposed for any crime unless—may it never happen—I should deviate from the Faith. For the prudence of the holy bishops entrusted the judgment and the deposition even of Julian the Apostate not to themselves, but to God alone. The true pope Saint Peter also exclaims, "Fear God, honor the king" [1 Pet 2:17]. You, however, since you do not fear God, dishonor me, ordained of Him.

Wherefore, when Saint Paul gave no quarter to an angel from heaven if the angel should preach heterodoxy, he did not except you who are now teaching heterodoxy throughout the earth.

Saint Gregory

In chapter 11, we read about Pope Saint Gregory the Great (Gregory I). As we learned from the writings of Saint Bede the Venerable, Gregory I was among the most highly regarded popes in history. In this chapter, Henry IV claims that Gregory VII is arrogant and disrespectful for taking the name of the great and sainted Pope Gregory I.

Heterodoxy

Heterodoxy means to teach something that is clearly false doctrine or blatantly against the norms of the Christian faith.

For he says, "If anyone, either I or an angel from heaven, preach any other gospel unto you than that which we have preached unto you, let him be accursed" [Gal 1:18]. Descend, therefore, condemned by this anathema and by the common judgment of all our bishops and of ourself. Relinquish the Apostolic See which you have arrogated. Let another mount the throne of Saint Peter, another who will not cloak violence with religion but who will teach the pure doctrine of Saint Peter.

I, Henry, King by the grace of God, together with all our bishops, say to you: Descend! Descend!

Chapter 16

"We Adore Thee, Lord Jesus Christ": The Last Words of the Tiny Friar

"The Testament of Saint Francis"

Who Wrote It?

Saint Francis was the son a wealthy clothing merchant in Assisi, Italy. The pride and joy of his father, Francis possessed the skills and talent to continue the family business. However, Francis chose a radical departure from the life of an upper-middle-class businessman.

As a young man, Francis became a soldier and went off to war. In one particular battle, his troop suffered a sound defeat and Francis was taken as a prisoner of war. After months in a dungeon, Francis returned home to recuperate. While recovering, Francis reflected on the direction of his life. During that time, God revealed to Francis that he would experience the greatest joy by embracing poverty and service to the poor as Jesus did.

The people of Assisi ridiculed such a radical following of the Gospel. However, others were attracted to a life of complete devotion to Jesus and his service. Francis soon found himself at the center of a movement—the *Frati Minori*, or in English, the "Little Brothers."

The order began with just a few Little Brothers, or friars, who lived in unfurnished mud huts. The order had no money, and the friars were not allowed to beg for any, but they could beg for items they needed, such as food, clothing, and materials for their ministry. The order's extreme commitment to poverty was, in Francis's mind, essential to remaining faithful to God's call to serve the poor and to preach conversion.

When Was It Written?

During the last two years of his life, Saint Francis endured many illnesses and physical suffering—as though his body had no more to give. In the last days of his life, in October 1226, Francis wrote this testament as he prepared for death.

Why Was It Written?

The small group of Little Brothers eventually grew to over 3,000 friars. With such growth, Francis spent much of his last years dealing with the bureaucratic needs of a growing community and struggling to hold to the vision of absolute poverty. As he was dying, Francis wrote his testament as a clear directive on how he thought the order should be run. The tone of the testament is strong and restrictive. Francis must have felt that elements in the Little Brothers would compromise the original vision. He insisted that the friars strictly obey the way of life set forth in the Rule of Saint Francis.

Why Is It Still Important Today?

Saint Francis of Assisi is one of the best-loved, most well-known saints of history. People throughout Christianity, and beyond, revere him. His testament might seem restrictive and perhaps extreme, but like everything else in his life, it flowed from Francis's love for Jesus. Francis emulated Christ in ways few can ever approach. His words, written at the close of his life, are a glimpse into the mind of a saint and an inspiration for living the Gospel more faithfully each day.

Primary Source: "The Testament of Saint Francis"

Thus did the Lord grant to me, Friar Francis, to begin to do penance: that when I was exceedingly in (my) sins, to see the lepers seemed a bitter thing to me. And the Lord Himself led me among them and I worked mercy with them. And when I was fleeing from them, because that seemed to me a bitter thing, it was changed for me into sweetness of soul and body; and afterwards I stayed for a little while and (then)

I went forth from the world (saeculum). And the Lord granted me such faith in churches, that thus I would pray simply and say: We adore Thee, Lord Jesus Christ, and for all Thy churches, which are in the whole world, we also bless Thee, because by Thy Holy Cross Thou has redeemed the world. Afterwards the Lord granted me and grants so much faith in priests, who live according to the form of the Holy Roman Church, on account of their state (in life), that if they would stir up a persecution against me, I want to have recourse to them. Even if I would have as much wisdom, as Solomon had, and would come upon the little poor priests of this age, in the parishes, where they linger, I do not wish to preach beyond their will. And they and all other (clerics) I want to fear, love (amor), and honor, as my lords. And I do not want to consider sin in them, because I discern in them the Son of God, and they are my lords. And I do (that) on account of this, because I see nothing corporally in this age of the Most High Son of God Himself, except His Most Holy Body and Most Holy Blood, which they receive and which they alone minister to others. And these Most Holy Mysteries I want above all things to honor, to venerate and to be placed in precious places. Wherever I will have found written the Most Holy Names and His words in unlawful places, I want to gather them together and I beg, that they are gathered together and placed together in an honorable place. And all theologians and those, who minister the most sacred divine words, we ought to honor and venerate, as those who minister to us spirit and life (cf. Jn 6:64).

And after the Lord gave me some friars, no one showed me, what I ought to do, but the Most High Himself revealed to me, that I ought to live according to the form of the Holy Gospel. And I had it written in a few words and simply and the Lord Pope confirmed it for me. And those who were coming to receive life, used to give "all that they possibly had" (Tob 1,3) to the poor; and they used to be content with one tunic, patched inside and out, with a cord and breeches. And we did not use to want to have more. We clerics used to say the Office along with the other clergy, the lay brothers used to say the Pater Noster; and we used to remain quite freely in the churches. And we used to be idiots and subject to all. And I used to work with my hands, and I want to work; and all the other brothers I firmly want, that they work at their job, because this pertains to honesty. Those who do not know how, let them learn, not for the sake of the cupidity to receive a price for work, but for the sake of the example (it gives) and to repel idleness. And when the price for the work would not be given to us, let us have recourse to the table of the Lord, by asking for alms door to door. The Lord revealed to me a greeting, that we are to say: "The Lord grant you peace!" Let all the friars beware of themselves, so that they receive almost none of the churches, the poor tiny dwellings and all (the buildings), which are constructed on their behalf, unless they would be, (such) as befits holy poverty, which we have promised in the Rule, always boarding there as exiles and pilgrims (cf. 1 Pet 2:11). I firmly precept all the friars by obedience, that wherever they are, they do not dare to seek any letter in the Roman Curia, by means of themselves nor by an interposed person, nor on behalf of a church nor on behalf of another place nor under the appearance of preaching nor on behalf of a persecution of their bodies; but wherever they have not been received, let them flee into another land to do penance with the blessing of God.

Divine Office

The *Divine Office* is also referred to as the "Liturgy of the Hours." The Office is prayed at set times during the day as a way to make the entire day holy. Each liturgy praises God through the Psalms, the reading of the sacred Scriptures, and prayers of intercession.

And I firmly want to obey the Minister general of this fraternity and any guardian, whom it will have pleased him to give me. And I want to be so captive in his hands, that I would not be able to go or do beyond obedience and his will, because he is my lord. And although I am simple and infirm, nevertheless I want to always have a cleric, who will perform the Office for me, as it is contained in the Rule. And all the other friars are bound to likewise obey their guardians and perform the Office according to the Rule. And those, who would be found, that do not perform the Office according to the Rule, and want to vary it in another manner, or are not Catholics, let all the friars, wherever they are, be bound by obedience, that wherever they have found any of these, they ought to present them before the nearest custos of that place, where they found him. And let the custos be firmly bound by obedience to guard him strongly, just like a man in chains day and night, so that he cannot be snatched from their hands, until he in person presents him into the hands of his minister. And let the minister be firmly bound by obedience to send him by means of such friars, that day and night guard him as a man in chains, until they present him before the lord of Ostia, who is the lord, protector and corrector of the whole fraternity. And let friars not say: "This is another Rule," because this is a remembrance, an admonition, an exhortation and my testament, which I, tiny Friar Francis, make for you, my blest friars, for the sake of this, that we might observe the Rule, which we have promised the Lord, in a more Catholic way.

And let the Minister General and all the other ministers and custodes be bound by obedience, not to add to these words nor take away. And let them have this writing with them always, next to the Rule. And in all the chapters that are convened, when they read the Rule, let them also read these words. And all my friars, cleric and lay, I firmly precept by obedience, to not place glosses upon the Rule, not even by saying in these words: "Thus they intend to be understood." But as the Lord granted me simply and purely to dictate and write the Rule and these words, so you should understand them simply and without gloss and observe them with holy work until the end. And whoever has observed these, may he be filled in heaven with the blessing of the Most High Father and on earth with the blessing of His Beloved (dilectio) Son with the Most Holy Spirit and all the Virtues of Heaven and all the saints. And I Friar Francis, your tiny servant, in as much as I am able, confirm for you, inside and out, that most holy blessing.

Chapter 17

Gentle and Powerful:
The First Woman Doctor of the Church

Letters to Pope Gregory XI

Who Wrote It?

Saint Catherine of Siena was born in the central Italian city of Siena in 1347 and died in Rome in 1380. The youngest of many children born into a lower-middle-class family, Catherine devoted herself to Jesus at an early age. In her thirty-three years of life, she experienced the heights of mystical prayer and the hard work of serving the poorest people. Catherine was also a prolific writer. Through her writings, prayer, and service, Catherine tried to reform the Church. In 1970 she was named a doctor of the Church.

When Was It Written?

The letters in this chapter were written between 1376 and 1377, at a time when the papacy was as much a political power as a religious one. For a seventy-four-year period, Europe had experienced

Doctor of the Church

A doctor of the Church is one whose teaching has had such influence that she or he has become an especially important figure in Christian history. To date, only thirty-three people have been given the title and only three are women. Saint Catherine of Siena and Saint Teresa of Ávila were so named in 1970 by Pope Paul VI. In 1977, Pope John Paul II named Saint Térèse of Lisieux a doctor of the Church.

a growing instability due, in part, to the Pope's residence at Avignon, France.

Why Was It Written?

In 1309 Pope Clement V moved the Church's government from Rome to Avignon, creating a theological problem because the bishop of Rome, the Pope, no longer lived in Rome. But the move also created a political problem. At the time, England and France were engaged in a long, bitter war, as were different papal states in Italy. Many Europeans were troubled that the Pope moved to France during that time. The Pope appeared to be backing France in the war. And without the Pope's presence in Italy, no one was in control in the papal states.

Catherine was not concerned with politics, but she recognized that political instability was threatening the spiritual mission of the Church. Through her letters, she raised Pope Gregory XI's courage to oppose the influential French cardinals of Avignon and return the papacy to Rome. Even after his return, the Pope's resolve seemed less than it might have been, and Catherine was bold in asserting what she believed to be God's will.

Why Is It Still Important Today?

Saint Catherine of Siena was forceful in telling the Pope and other important officials how they ought to behave. In her letters, she addressed the Pope humbly and tenderly. Yet, she spoke candidly and directly, qualities that might seem disrespectful if they came from people without Catherine's capacity for total love.

In naming Catherine a doctor of the Church, Pope Paul VI noted her "charism of exhortation"—a gift few possess with such complete devotion as Catherine's to the will of God. Catherine's commitment to God and love of all God's people shines through her exhortations. Her obedience to God's will, even if it meant confronting powerful people, is a strong example when compromise and manipulation seem like an easier path.

Primary Source: Letters to Pope Gregory XI

Letter to Pope Gregory XI Before He Returns the Papacy to Rome

In the Name of Jesus Christ crucified and of sweet Mary:

Most holy and blessed father in Christ sweet Jesus: your poor unworthy little daughter Catherine comforts you in His precious Blood, with desire to see you free from any servile fear. For I consider that a timorous man cuts short the vigour of holy resolves and good desire, and so I have prayed, and shall pray, sweet and good Jesus that He free you from all servile fear, and that holy fear alone remain. May ardour of charity be in you, in such wise as shall prevent you from hearing the voice of incarnate demons, and heeding the counsel of perverse counsellors, settled in self-love, who, as I understand, want to alarm you, so as to prevent your return, saying, "You will die." And I tell you on behalf of Christ crucified, most sweet and holy father, not to fear for any reason whatsoever. Come in security: trust you in Christ sweet Jesus: for, doing what you ought, God will be above you, and there will be no one who shall be against you. Up, father, like a man! For I tell you that you have no need to fear. You ought to come; come, then. Come gently, without any fear. And if any at home wish to hinder you, say to them bravely, as Christ said when St. Peter, through tenderness, wished to draw Him back from going to His passion: Christ turned to him, saying, "Get thee behind Me, Satan; thou art an offence to Me, seeking the things which are of men, and not those which are of God. Wilt thou not that I fulfil the will of My Father?" Do you likewise, sweetest father, following Him as His vicar, deliberating and deciding by yourself, and saying to those who would hinder you, "If my life should be spent a thousand times, I wish to fulfil the will of my Father." Although bodily life be laid down for it, yet seize on the life of grace and the means of winning it for ever. Now comfort you and fear not, for you have no need. Put on the armour of the most holy Cross, which is the safety and the life of Christians. Let talk who will, and hold you firm in your holy resolution. My father, Fra Raimondo, said to me on your behalf that I was to pray God to see whether you were to meet with an obstacle, and I had already prayed about it, before and after Holy Communion, and I saw neither death nor any peril. Those perils are invented by the men who counsel you. Believe, and trust you in Christ sweet Jesus. I hope that God will not despise so many prayers, made with so ardent desire, and with many tears and sweats. I say no more. Remain in the holy and sweet grace of God. Pardon me, pardon me. Jesus Christ crucified be with you. Sweet Jesus, Jesus Love.

Babbo

Babbo is an Italian word that means "papa" or "daddy."

Letter to Pope Gregory XI After the Papacy Returns to Rome

In the Name of Jesus Christ crucified and of sweet Mary:

Most holy and sweet father, your poor unworthy daughter Catherine in Christ sweet Jesus, commends herself to you in His precious Blood: with desire to see you a manly man, free from any fear or fleshly love toward yourself, or toward any creature related to you in the flesh; since I perceive in the sweet Presence of God that nothing so hinders your holy, good desire and so serves to hinder the honour of God and the exaltation and reform of Holy Church, as this. Therefore, my soul desires with immeasurable love that God by His infinite mercy may take from you all passion and lukewarmness of heart, and re-form you another man, by forming in you anew a burning and ardent desire; for in no other way could you fulfil the will of God and the desire of His servants. Alas, alas, sweetest "Babbo" mine, pardon my presumption in what I have said to you and am saying; I am constrained by the Sweet Primal Truth to say it. His will, father, is this, and thus demands of you. It demands that you execute justice on the abundance of many iniquities committed by those who are fed and pastured in the garden of Holy Church; declaring that brutes should not be fed with the food of men. Since He has given you authority and you have assumed it, you should use your virtue and power: and if you are not willing to use it, it would be better for you to resign what you have assumed; more honour to God and health to your soul would it be.

Another demand that His will makes is this: He wills that you make peace with all Tuscany, with which you are at strife; securing from all your wicked sons who have rebelled against you whatever is possible to secure without war—but punishing them as a father ought to punish a son who has wronged him. Moreover, the sweet goodness of God demands from you that you give full authority to those who ask you to make ready for the Holy Crusade—that thing which appears impossible to you, and possible to the sweet goodness of God, who has ordained it, and wills that so it be. Beware, as you hold your life dear, that you commit no negligence in this, nor treat as jests the works of the Holy Spirit, which are demanded from you because you can do them. If you want justice, you can execute it. You can have peace, withdrawing from the perverse pomps and delights of the world, preserving only the honor of God and the due of Holy Church. Authority also you have to give peace to those who ask you for it. Then, since you are not poor but rich—you who bear in your hand the keys of Heaven, to whom you open it is open, and to whom you shut it is shut—if you do not do this, you would be rebuked by God. I, if I were in your place, should fear lest divine judgment come upon me. Therefore I beg you most gently on behalf of Christ crucified to be obedient to the will of God, for I know that you want and desire no other thing than to do His will, that this sharp rebuke fall not upon you: "Cursed be thou, for the time and the strength entrusted to thee thou hast not used." I believe, father, by the goodness of God, and also taking hope from your holiness, that you will so act that this will not fall upon you.

I say no more. Pardon me, pardon me; for the great love which I bear to your salvation, and my great grief when I see the contrary, makes me speak so. Willingly would I have said it to your own person, fully to unburden my conscience. When it shall please your Holiness that I come to you, I will come willingly. So do that I may not appeal to Christ crucified from you; for to no other can I appeal, for there is no greater on earth. Remain in the holy and sweet grace of God. I ask you humbly for your benediction. Sweet Jesus, Jesus Love.

Chapter 18

Revival of Prayer:
A Springtime for Spirituality

The Imitation of Christ

Who Wrote It?

Thomas á Kempis was born about 1379 in the village of Kempen in what is modern-day Germany. At the young age of thirteen, Thomas went to school in Holland. While there, he was introduced to a new movement that wanted to recapture the spirit and fervor of the earliest Christians. Following in the footsteps of his older brother, Thomas joined the movement. After a life of devotion to God and service to neighbor, Thomas died in 1471.

When Was It Written?

Although the exact date is uncertain, most historians believe *The Imitation of Christ* was written in 1425.

Why Was It Written?

In the fourteenth and fifteenth centuries, much of Europe and the Church hierarchy were scandalously corrupt. However, among many of the people of Europe, the human longing for God endured. That irrepressible desire for God caused many reform movements to spring up and attract large numbers of followers. One such movement was the Brethren of the Common Life, founded by Geert de Groote. Thomas á

Kempis, one of the Brethren of the Common Life, wrote *The Imitation of Christ* to provide a guide for those who wanted to develop an intimate and single-hearted friendship with Jesus Christ.

Why Is It Still Important Today?

The Imitation of Christ is probably second only to the Bible as the most-read Christian work in history. For more than 500 years, the work has been an inspiration to those seeking to live out the Gospel call more faithfully. *The Imitation of Christ* dives to the heart of Christianity. Being a disciple of Jesus is a matter of loving Jesus and having Jesus as an intimate friend. *The Imitation of Christ* holds a mirror up to a Christian's heart to reveal the Christian's loves. It asks: "What is loved more than Jesus? What can satisfy the desires of the human heart more than Jesus?" Because of its place in Christian spirituality, *The Imitation of Christ* has endured as an important reading in the history of the Church.

Primary Source: *The Imitation of Christ*

The Sixth Chapter: The Joy of a Good Conscience

The glory of a good man is the testimony of a good conscience. Therefore, keep your conscience good and you will always enjoy happiness, for a good conscience can bear a great deal and can bring joy even in the midst of adversity. But an evil conscience is ever restive and fearful.

Sweet shall be your rest if your heart does not reproach you.

Do not rejoice unless you have done well. Sinners never experience true interior joy or peace, for "there is no peace to the wicked," says the Lord. Even if they say: "We are at peace, no evil shall befall us and no one dares to hurt us," do not believe them; for the wrath of God will arise quickly, and their deeds will be brought to naught and their thoughts will perish.

To glory in adversity is not hard for the man who loves, for this is to glory in the cross of the Lord. But the glory given or received of men is short lived, and the glory of the world is ever companioned by sorrow. The glory of the good, however, is in their conscience and not in the lips of men, for the joy of the just is from God and in God, and their gladness is founded on truth.

The man who longs for the true, eternal glory does not care for that of time; and he who seeks passing fame or does not in his heart despise it, undoubtedly cares little for the glory of heaven.

He who minds neither praise nor blame possesses great peace of heart and, if his conscience is good, he will easily be contented and at peace.

Praise adds nothing to your holiness, nor does blame take anything from it. You are what you are, and you cannot be said to be better than you are in God's sight. If you consider well what you are within, you will not care what men say about you. They look to appearances but God looks to the heart. They consider the deed but God weighs the motive.

It is characteristic of a humble soul always to do good and to think little of itself. It is a mark of great purity and deep faith to look for no consolation in created things. The man who desires no justification from without has clearly entrusted himself to God: "For not he who commendeth himself is approved," says St. Paul, "but he whom God commendeth."

To walk with God interiorly, to be free from any external affection—this is the state of the inward man.

The Seventh Chapter: Loving Jesus Above All Things

Blessed is he who appreciates what it is to love Jesus and who despises himself for the sake of Jesus. Give up all other love for His, since He wishes to be loved alone above all things.

Affection for creatures is deceitful and inconstant, but the love of Jesus is true and enduring. He who clings to a creature will fall with its frailty, but he who gives himself to Jesus will ever be strengthened.

Love Him, then; keep Him as a friend. He will not leave you as others do, or let you suffer lasting death. Sometime, whether you will or not, you will have to part with everything. Cling, therefore, to Jesus in life and death; trust yourself to the glory of Him who alone can help you when all others fail.

Your Beloved is such that He will not accept what belongs to another—He wants your heart for Himself alone, to be enthroned therein as King in His own right. If you but knew how to free yourself entirely from all creatures, Jesus would gladly dwell within you.

You will find, apart from Him, that nearly all the trust you place in men is a total loss. Therefore, neither confide in nor depend upon a wind-shaken reed, for "all flesh is grass" and all its glory, like the flower of grass, will fade away.

You will quickly be deceived if you look only to the outward appearance of men, and you will often be disappointed if you seek comfort and gain in them. If, however, you seek Jesus in all things, you will surely find Him. Likewise, if you seek yourself, you will find yourself—to your own ruin. For the man who does not seek Jesus does himself much greater harm than the whole world and all his enemies could ever do.

The Eighth Chapter: The Intimate Friendship of Jesus

When Jesus is near, all is well and nothing seems difficult. When He is absent, all is hard. When Jesus does not speak within, all other comfort is empty, but if He says only a word, it brings great consolation.

Did not Mary Magdalen rise at once from her weeping when Martha said to her: "The Master is come, and calleth for thee"? Happy is the hour when Jesus calls one from tears to joy of spirit.

How dry and hard you are without Jesus! How foolish and vain if you desire anything but Him! Is it not a greater loss than losing the whole world? For what, without Jesus, can the world give you? Life without Him is a relentless hell, but living with Him is a sweet paradise. If Jesus be with you, no enemy can harm you.

He who finds Jesus finds a rare treasure, indeed, a good above every good, whereas he who loses Him loses more than the whole world. The man who lives without Jesus is the poorest of the poor, whereas no one is so rich as the man who lives in His grace.

It is a great art to know how to converse with Jesus, and great wisdom to know how to keep Him. Be humble and peaceful, and Jesus will be with you. Be devout and calm, and He will remain with you. You may quickly drive Him away and lose His grace, if you turn back to the outside world. And, if you drive Him away and lose Him, to whom will you go and whom will you then seek as a friend? You cannot live well without a friend, and if Jesus be not your friend above all else, you will be very sad and desolate. Thus, you are acting foolishly if you trust or rejoice in any other. Choose the opposition of the whole world rather than offend Jesus. Of all those who are dear to you, let Him be your special love. Let all things be loved for the sake of Jesus, but Jesus for His own sake.

Jesus Christ must be loved alone with a special love for He alone, of all friends, is good and faithful. For Him and in Him you must love friends and foes alike, and pray to Him that all may know and love Him.

Never desire special praise or love, for that belongs to God alone Who has no equal. Never wish that anyone's affection be centered in you, nor let yourself be taken up with the love of anyone, but let Jesus be in you and in every good man. Be pure and free within, unentangled with any creature.

You must bring to God a clean and open heart if you wish to attend and see how sweet the Lord is. Truly you will never attain this happiness unless His grace prepares you and draws you on so that you may forsake all things to be united with Him alone.

When the grace of God comes to a man he can do all things, but when it leaves him he becomes poor and weak, abandoned, as it were, to affliction. Yet, in this condition he should not become dejected or despair. On the contrary, he should calmly await the will of God and bear whatever befalls him in praise of Jesus Christ, for after winter comes summer, after night, the day, and after the storm, a great calm.

Chapter 19

The Revolutionary Monk:
The Protestant Reformation Begins

Writings from Martin Luther

Who Wrote It?

Martin Luther was born in Eisleben, Germany, in 1483 and died there in 1546. When Luther was a young man, he was struck by lightning during a violent thunderstorm. Imagining the storm to be a small taste of his fate should he die, he prayed to Saint Anne and promised to devote his life to God if he survived. He survived and, in fulfillment of his promise, he became an Augustinian monk. However, he felt burdened by performing "good works" to appease God.

In an attempt to give Luther a more constructive outlook on his faith and his life, the superior of the monastery urged Luther to study the sacred Scriptures. Ultimately, Luther became an expert Scripture scholar and teacher, particularly on the letters of Saint Paul.

When Luther was in his thirties, he had a powerful experience of God's love and acceptance. From that experience, Luther understood that faith is the source of holiness, not good works. Salvation is something God gives freely to humans; it is not something earned. That experience led him to challenge the Catholic faith. He believed that indulgences, sacraments, and obedience to the Church's teaching authority were attempts to earn salvation rather than channels of salvation.

When Was It Written?

"An Open Letter to the Christian Nobility of the German Nation" was written in 1520. "An Introduction to St. Paul's Letter to the Romans" was written in 1522.

Why Was It Written?

Originally, Martin Luther did not seek to break from the Catholic Church. Rather, he wanted to reform the Church. At first, Luther did not draw much attention, and Rome more or less ignored him. However, as more people began to discuss Luther's ideas, Rome took notice and sought to have Luther modify some of his positions. In the end, Luther was unable to recant anything. Luther wrote "An Open Letter to the Christian Nobility of the German Nation Concerning the Reform of the Christian Estate" when he realized his split with the Roman Catholic Church was permanent. It said that he would not recant anything he had stated.

After the publication of "An Open Letter," along with two other famous treatises in the same year—"The Babylonian Captivity of the Church" and "On the Freedom of a Christian"—Luther's popularity and power grew within Germany and eventually in much of Europe. He put his skill as a Scripture scholar to work in writing "An Introduction to St. Paul's Letter to the Romans." In that work, he clearly outlined the "lightning strike" insight he had about the role of faith in our salvation, as opposed to good works alone.

Why Is It Still Important Today?

Many of the reforms Luther called for were reforms the Church would have (and did) eventually implemented anyway. In fact, a major reconciliation occurred on October 31, 1999, when the "Joint Declaration on the Doctrine of Justification" was signed by the Lutheran World Federation and the Catholic Church. After almost 500 years, Martin Luther's invitation to discuss and debate the issue of justification was finally answered. Reading Luther's writings today, we can see what seems to be an unnecessary belligerence and antagonism. But if we look past that element, we also see a clear and reasoned argument for reform that has as its deepest motivation a devoted concern for the people of God. The Catholic Church acknowledges that the Church is in constant need of renewal. These writings are most important for the Church's history, but they also hold a lesson for the Church in future years. It is vital for Christians to both reform the Church and seek the unity of the Body of Christ.

Primary Source: Writings from Martin Luther

Open Letter to the Christian Nobility of the German Nation

To the Esteemed and Reverend Master
Nicholas von Amsdorf
Licentiate Of holy Scripture and Canon at Wittenberg,
my special and kind friend;
Doctor Martin Luther.

The grace and peace of God be with thee, esteemed and reverend dear sir and friend.

The time to keep silence has passed and the time to (Eccl 3:7) speak is come, as saith Ecclesiastes. I have followed out intention and brought together some matters touching the reform of the Christian Estate, to be laid before the Christian Nobility of the German Nation, in the hope that may deign to help His Church through the efforts of the laity, since the clergy, to whom this task more properly belongs, have grown quite indifferent. I am sending the whole thing to your Reverence, that you may pass judgment on it and, if necessary, improve it.

I know full well that I shall not escape the charge of presumption in that I, a despised monk, venture to address such high and great Estates on matters of such moment, and to give advice to people of such high intelligence. I shall offer no apologies, no matter who may chide me. Perchance I owe my God and the world another pie of folly, and I have now made up my mind honestly to pay that debt, if I can do so, and for once to become court jester; if I fail, I still have one advantage—no one need buy me a cap or cut me my comb. It is a question which one will put the bells on the other. I must fulfill the proverb, "Whatever the world does, a monk must be it, even if he has to be painted in." More than once a fool has spoken wisely, and wise men often have been arrant (1 Cor 3:18) fools, as Paul says, "If any one will be wise, let him become a fool." Moreover since I am not only a fool, but also a sworn doctor of Holy Scripture, I am glad for the chant to fulfill my doctor's oath in this fool's way.

I pray you, make my excuses to the moderately intelligent, for I know not how to earn the grace and favor of the immoderately intelligent, though I have often sought to do with great pains. Henceforth I neither desire nor regard their favor. God help us to seek not our own glory, but His alone! Amen.

Wittenberg, in the house of the Augustinians, on the Eve of St. John the Baptist (June 23rd), in the year fifteen hundred and twenty.

Martin Luther's Definition of Faith: An excerpt from "An Introduction to St. Paul's Letter to the Romans,"

Faith is not what some people think it is. Their human dream is a delusion. Because they observe that faith is not followed by good works or a better life, they fall into error, even though they speak and hear much about faith. "Faith is not enough," they say, "You must do good works, you must be pious to be saved.'" They think that, when you hear the gospel, you start working, creating by your own strength a thankful heart which says, "I believe." That is what they think true faith is. But, because this is a human idea, a dream, the heart never learns anything from it, so it does nothing and reform doesn't come from this "faith," either.

Instead, faith is God's work in us, that changes us and gives new birth from God (John 1:13). It kills the Old Adam and makes us completely different people. It changes our hearts, our spirits, our thoughts and all our powers. It brings the Holy Spirit with it. Yes, it is a living, creative, active and powerful thing, this faith. Faith cannot help doing good works constantly. It doesn't stop to ask if good works ought to be done, but before anyone asks, it already has done them and continues to do them without ceasing. Anyone who does not do good works in this manner is an unbeliever. He stumbles around and looks for faith and good works, even though he does not know what faith or good works are. Yet he gossips and chatters about faith and good works with many words.

Faith is a living, bold trust in God's grace, so certain of God's favor that it would risk death a thousand times trusting in it. Such confidence and knowledge of God's grace makes you happy, joyful and bold in your relationship to God and all creatures. The Holy Spirit makes this happen through faith. Because of it, you freely, willingly and joyfully do good to everyone, serve everyone, suffer all kinds of things, love and praise the God who has shown you such grace. Thus, it is just as impossible to separate faith and works as it is to separate heat and light from fire! Therefore, watch out for your own false ideas and guard against good-for-nothing gossips, who think they're smart enough to define faith and works, but really are the greatest of fools. Ask God to work faith in you, or you will remain forever without faith, no matter what you wish, say or can do.

Chapter 20

"What Is Necessary Is a Different Approach": The Catholic Reformation

The Way of Perfection

Who Wrote It?

Saint Teresa of Ávila was born in Spain in 1515 and given the name Teresa de Cepeda y Ahumada. She was born to a wealthy family and, as a child, learned how to be a socialite. When she was sixteen, she became overly romantic with a suitor, and her father responded by sending her to a convent finishing school. He did not intend for his daughter to become a nun, but against her father's wishes, twenty-year-old Teresa secretly entered the Carmelite order.

As a nun, Teresa did all that was expected of her, but she was not particularly devout. She led a fairly comfortable life in a well-financed convent, and she reported that she had difficulty praying. When she was nearly forty, she had a life-changing experience, which she described as being engulfed by Christ.

Doctor of the Church

A doctor of the Church is one whose teaching has had such influence that she or he has become an especially important figure in Christian history. To date, only thirty-three people have been given the title and only three are women. Saint Catherine of Siena and Saint Teresa of Ávila were so named in 1970 by Pope Paul VI. In 1997, Pope John Paul II named Saint Térèse of Lisieux a doctor of the Church.

That experience marked the beginning of her mystical life and her efforts to reform the Carmelite order. She eventually succeeded in separating her reform movement, known as the *Discalced* (barefoot or unshod) Carmelites, from the older Carmelite order. She went on to found seventeen convents and has been named a doctor of the Church.

When Was It Written?

Saint Teresa wrote *The Way of Perfection* during the Catholic Reformation of the mid-1560s.

Why Was It Written?

Saint Teresa wrote *The Way of Perfection* during a time of controversy. While she was reforming the Carmelite order, the (Protestant) Reformation was rushing through the rest of Europe. *The Way of Perfection* begins with Teresa's description of why she thought a new reform or a new approach was needed. That is, she wanted to increase people's faith and devotion to minimize the damage done by Martin Luther and the other Reformation leaders in the Catholic Church.

The Catholic Reformation

From the early 1500s until the mid-1600s a broad movement was at work in the Catholic Church. This movement sought to reform the Church by correcting the corruption and abuses present in the Church. Reformers such as Saint Ignatius of Loyola and Saint Teresa of Ávila wanted to call the Church away from the pursuit of money and political gain and back to a zealous love for Jesus.

Teresa's new approach was a guide to prayer, especially for new nuns who joined the Discalced Carmelites. Teresa's spiritual counselors asked her to write of her experiences of prayer. She was faithful to this request and fit her writing time into the late hours of the night because administering the order and founding new convents took up most of her time.

In *The Way of Perfection,* Teresa explains the requirements for attaining spiritual perfection through prayer, and she identifies four stages of prayer. The first stage is meditation. The second stage is quiet. The third stage is the repose of the soul. The final stage is perfect union with God, which she describes as rapture.

Why Is It Still Important Today?

Saint Teresa's writings are the principle reason she was declared a doctor of the Church. Her works, especially *The Way of Perfection,* are considered spiritual classics on the practice of prayer. She gives concrete, practical advice and guidance that moves Christians along the way of perfection.

Primary Source: *The Way of Perfection*

When I began to take the first steps toward founding this monastery (for the reasons given in the book I mentioned that I wrote and also because of some great favors from the Lord through which I learned that He would be greatly served in this house), it was not my intention that there be so much external austerity or that the house have no income; on the contrary, I would have desired the possibility that nothing be lacking. In sum, my intention was the intention of the weak and wretched person that I am—although I did have some good motives besides those involving my own comfort.

At that time news reached me of the harm being done in France and of the havoc the Lutherans had caused and how much this miserable sect was growing. The news distressed me greatly, and, as though I could do something or were something, I cried to the Lord and begged Him that I might remedy so much evil. It seemed to me that I would have given a thousand lives to save one soul out of the many that were being lost there. I realized I was a woman and wretched and in capable of doing any of the useful things I desired to do in the service of the Lord. All my longing was and still is that since He has so many enemies and so few friends that these few friends be good ones. As a result I resolved to do the little that was in my power; that is, to follow the evangelical counsels as perfectly as I could and strive that these few persons who live here do the same. I did this trusting in the great goodness of God, who never fails to help anyone who is determined to give up everything for Him. My trust was that if these Sisters matched the ideal my desires had set for them, my faults would not have much strength in the midst of so many virtues; and I could thereby please the Lord in some way. Since we would all be occupied in prayer for those who are the defenders of the Church and for preachers and for learned men who protect her from attack, we could help as much as possible this Lord of mine who is so roughly treated by those for whom He has done so much good; it seems these traitors would want Him to be crucified again and that He have no place to lay His head.

O my Redeemer, my heart cannot bear these thoughts without becoming terribly grieved. What is the matter with Christians nowadays? Must it always be those who owe You the most who afflict You? Those for whom You performed the greatest works, those You have chosen for Your friends, with whom You walk and commune by means of Your sacraments? Aren't they satisfied with the torments You have suffered for them?

> ## Evangelical Counsels
> The Evangelical Counsels are the vows of poverty, obedience, and chastity.

Indeed, my Lord, one who withdraws from the world nowadays is not doing anything. Since the world so little appreciates You, what do we expect? Do we perhaps deserve to be treated better? Have we perhaps done better toward those in the world that they would keep us in their friendship? What is this? What do we now expect, those of us who through the goodness of the Lord are freed of that contagious, scabby sore, that sect whose followers already belong to the devil? Indeed, they have won punishment with their own hands and have easily earned eternal fire with their pleasures. That's their worry! Still, my heart breaks to see how many souls are lost. Though I can't grieve so much over the evil already done—that is irreparable—I would not want to see more of them lost each day.

O my Sisters in Christ, help me beg these things of the Lord. This is why He has gathered you together here. This is your vocation. These must be the business matters you're engaged in. These must be the things you desire, the things you weep about; these must be the objects of your petitions—not, my Sisters, the business matters of the world. For I laugh at and am even distressed about the things they come here to ask us to pray for: to ask His Majesty for wealth and money—and this is done by persons who I wish would ask Him for the grace to trample everything underfoot. They are well intentioned, and in the end we pray for their intentions because of their devotion—although for myself I don't think the Lord ever hears me when I pray for these things. The world is all in flames; they want to sentence Christ again, so to speak, since they raise a thousand false witnesses against Him; they want to ravage His Church—and are we to waste time asking for things that if God were to give them we'd have one soulless in heaven? No, my Sisters, this is not the time to be discussing with God matters that have little importance.

Indeed, were I not to consider the human weakness that is consoled by receiving help in time of need (and it is good that we help in so far as we can), I'd be happy only if people understood that these are not the things they should be begging God for with so much care. . . .

To return to the main reason the Lord brought us together in this house and why I have greatly desired that we live so as to please His Majesty, I want to speak of helping to remedy the great evils I have seen. Human forces are not sufficient to stop the spread of this fire caused by these heretics, even though people have tried to see if with the force of arms they could remedy all the evil that is making such progress. It has seemed to me that what is necessary is a different approach, the approach of a lord when in time of war his land is overrun with enemies and he finds himself restricted on all sides. He withdraws to a city that he has well fortified and from there sometimes strikes his foe. Those who are in the city, being chosen people, are such that they can do more by themselves than many cowardly soldiers can. And often victory is won in this way. At least, even though victory is not won, these chosen people are not conquered. For since they have no traitor, they cannot be conquered—unless through starvation. In this example the starvation cannot be such as to force them to surrender— to die, yes; but not to surrender.

But why have I said this? So that you understand, my Sisters, that what we must ask God is that in this little castle where there are already good Christians not one of us will go over to the enemy and that God will make the captains of this castle or city, who are the preachers and theologians, very advanced in the way of the Lord. Since most of them belong to religious orders, ask God that they advance very far in the perfection of religious life and their vocation; this is most necessary. For as I have said, it is the ecclesiastical, not the secular, arm that will save us. Since in neither the ecclesiastical nor the secular arm can we be of any help to our King, let us strive to be the kind of persons whose prayers can be useful in helping those servants of God who through much toil have strengthened themselves with learning and a good life and have labored so as now to help the Lord.

Chapter 21

"Nor Should They Be in Any Way Enslaved": Europeans Encounter the West

Inter Caetera

Who Wrote It?

Pope Alexander VI, a Spaniard, was the Pope from August 11, 1492, until his death on August 18, 1503.

When Was It Written?

Inter Caetera was written on May 4, 1493, very soon after Christopher Columbus landed on the islands we now know as the Bahamas.

Why Was It Written?

In 1492, under the flag of Spain, Christopher Columbus set sail in hopes of finding a new passage to Asia and India. When Columbus landed in what would be called the Americas, he claimed the land for Spain. However, Portugal claimed the right to colonize the new territory based on previous papal pronouncements. In the face of such a conflict, King Ferdinand of Spain

Papal Bull

A papal bull is a statement or declaration from the Pope. While any writing from the pope is important, a bull is not held in the same light as other papal writings, such as encyclicals. This kind of declaration receives its name from *bulla*, the Latin word for the seal attached to the document.

requested that Pope Alexander VI, a native Spaniard and a personal friend, write a new bull. The bull *Inter Caetera* gave Spain exclusive and unlimited rights in the New World.

Why Is It Still Important Today?

Pope Alexander VI's bull was interpreted by Spain as a license to do whatever it wanted in the Americas, an interpretation that led to the abuse, enslavement, and forced conversion of massive numbers of native tribes, nations, and peoples. Although evangelization is always the first duty of the Church, it cannot be used as an excuse for mistreatment.

Native groups have called for the revocation of *Inter Caetera* because they see the papal bull as the foundation for the oppression they have suffered since Columbus explored the Americas. At the 1993 Parliament of the World's Religions, a gathering of indigenous people issued the following statement:

> We call upon the people of conscience in the Roman Catholic hierarchy to persuade Pope John II to formally revoke the Inter Caetera Bull of May 4, 1493, which will restore our fundamental human rights. That Papal document called for our Nations and Peoples to be subjugated so the Christian Empire and its doctrines would be propagated. The U.S. Supreme Court ruling Johnson v. McIntosh 8 Wheat 543 (in 1823) adopted the same principle of subjugation expressed in the Inter Caetera Bull. This Papal Bull has been, and continues to be, devastating to our religions, our cultures, and the survival of our populations.

It is important to read *Inter Caetera* to learn how its effects are still being felt by native peoples and to explore new ways the Church might continue to reach out and interact with native peoples in ways that honor and revere their cultures.

Primary Source: *Inter Caetera*

Alexander, bishop, servant of the servants of God, to the illustrious sovereigns, our very dear son in Christ, Ferdinand, king, and our very dear daughter in Christ, Isabella, queen of Castile, Leon, Aragon, Sicily, and Granada, health and apostolic benediction. Among other works well pleasing to the Divine Majesty and cherished of our heart, this assuredly ranks highest, that in our times especially the Catholic faith and the Christian religion be exalted and be everywhere increased and spread, that the health of souls be cared for and that barbarous nations be overthrown and brought to the faith itself. Wherefore inasmuch as by the favor of divine clemency, we, though of insufficient merits, have been called to this Holy See of Peter, recognizing that as true Catholic kings and princes, such as we have known you always to be, and as your illustrious deeds already known to almost the whole world declare, you not only eagerly desire but with every effort, zeal, and diligence, without regard to hardships, expenses, dangers, with the shedding even of your blood, are laboring to that end; recognizing also that you have long since dedicated to this purpose your whole soul and all your endeavors—as witnessed in these times with so much glory to the Divine Name in your recovery of the kingdom

Apostolic Benediction

As the person who continues the ministry of Saint Peter the Apostle, the Pope conveys a special blessing called the Apostolic Benediction.

Grenada and the Saracens

The Saracens were Muslims who occupied Grenada, a section of Spain. In *Inter Caetera*, Pope Alexander VI is praising Queen Isabella for driving the Saracens out of Grenada.

of Granada from the yoke of the Saracens—we therefore are rightly led, and hold it as our duty, to grant you even of our own accord and in your favor those things whereby with effort each day more hearty you may be enabled for the honor of God himself and the spread of the Christian rule to carry forward your holy and praiseworthy purpose so pleasing to immortal God. We have indeed learned that you, who for a long time had intended to seek out and discover certain islands and mainlands remote and unknown and not hitherto discovered by others, to the end that you might bring to the worship of our Redeemer and the profession of the Catholic faith their residents and inhabitants, having been up to the present time greatly engaged in the siege and recovery of the kingdom itself of Granada were unable to accomplish this holy and praiseworthy purpose; but the said kingdom having at length been regained, as was pleasing to the Lord, you, with the wish to fulfill your desire, chose our beloved son, Christopher Columbus, a man assuredly worthy and of the highest recommendations and fitted for so great an undertaking, whom you furnished with ships and men equipped for like designs, not without the greatest hardships, dangers, and expenses, to make diligent quest for these remote and unknown mainlands and islands through the sea, where hitherto no one had sailed; and they at length, with divine aid and with the utmost diligence sailing in the ocean sea, discovered certain very remote islands and even mainlands that hitherto had not been discovered by others; wherein dwell very many peoples living in peace, and, as reported, going unclothed, and not eating flesh. Moreover, as your aforesaid envoys are of opinion, these very peoples living in the said islands and countries believe in one God, the Creator in heaven, and seem sufficiently disposed to embrace the Catholic faith and be trained in good morals. And it is hoped that, were they instructed, the name of the Savior, our Lord Jesus Christ, would easily be introduced into the said countries and islands. . . . Given at Rome, at St. Peter's, in the year of the incarnation of our Lord one thousand four hundred and ninety-three, the fourth of May, and the first year of our pontificate.

Sublimus Dei

Who Wrote It?

Pope Paul III, an Italian, was elected Pope on October 12, 1534, and died in Rome on November 10, 1549.

When Was It Written?

Sublimus Dei was written on May 29, 1537, when the colonization of the West by European nations was booming.

Why Was It Written?

Sublimus Dei, a document written to the entire Christian people, clearly opposes slavery and the abuse of native peoples during the colonization of the Americas. The document is written as a condemnation of those who would use the proclamation of the faith and the mission of evangelization as an excuse to enslave people.

Why Is It Still Important Today?

Sublimus Dei demonstrates the core teaching of the Church that all people are fully human and fully loved by God. The claim that people of another culture or race are less than human and can be denied their full rights and dignity is illegitimate. *Sublimus Dei* is a fundamental building block in the Church's social teaching.

Nevertheless, the document, which seems to suggest that the native peoples are without faith, needs to be read within the context of its time. At the time *Sublimus Dei* was written, some Europeans still used the perceived mandate of converting native peoples as an excuse for occupying the natives' lands.

Today, the Church understands its mission of evangelization as "a *respectful dialogue* with those who do not yet accept the Gospel" (*Catechism*, paragraph 856). Pope Paul VI articulated the teaching of the Church in "Declaration on the Relation of the Church to Non-Christian Religions":

> No foundation therefore remains for any theory or practice that leads to discrimination between man and man or people and people, so far as their human dignity and the rights flowing from it are concerned.

> The Church reproves, as foreign to the mind of Christ, any discrimination against men or harassment of them because of their race, color, condition of life, or religion.

Primary Source: *Sublimus Dei*

To all faithful Christians to whom this writing may come, health in Christ our Lord and the apostolic benediction.

The sublime God so loved the human race that He created man in such wise that he might participate, not only in the good that other creatures enjoy, but endowed him with capacity to attain to the inaccessible and invisible Supreme Good and behold it face to face; and since man, according to the testimony of the sacred scriptures, has been created to enjoy eternal life and happiness, which none may obtain save through faith in our Lord Jesus Christ, it is necessary that he should possess the nature and faculties enabling him to receive that faith; and that whoever is thus endowed should be capable of receiving that same faith. Nor is it credible that any one should possess so little understanding as to desire the faith and yet be destitute of the most necessary faculty to enable him to receive it. Hence Christ, who is the Truth itself, that has never failed and can never fail, said to the preachers of the faith whom He chose for that office, "Go ye and teach all nations." He said all, without exception, for all are capable of receiving the doctrines of the faith.

The enemy of the human race, who opposes all good deeds in order to bring men to destruction, beholding and envying this, invented a means never before heard of, by which he might hinder the preaching of God's word of Salvation to the people: he inspired his satellites who, to please him, have not hesitated to publish abroad that the Indians of the West and the South, and other people of whom We have recent knowledge should be treated as dumb brutes created for our service, pretending that they are incapable of receiving the Catholic Faith.

We, who, though unworthy, exercise on earth the power of our Lord and seek with all our might to bring those sheep of His flock who are outside into the fold committed to our charge, consider, however, that the Indians are truly men and that they are not only capable of understanding the Catholic Faith but, according to our information, they desire exceedingly to receive it. Desiring to provide ample remedy for these evils, We define and declare by these Our letters, or by any translation thereof signed by any notary public and sealed with the seal of any ecclesiastical dignitary, to which the same credit shall be given as to the originals, that, notwithstanding whatever may have been or may be said to the contrary, the said Indians and all other people who may later be discovered by Christians, are by no means to be deprived of their liberty or the possession of their property, even though they be outside the faith of Jesus Christ; and that they may and should, freely and legitimately, enjoy their liberty and the possession of their property; nor should they be in any way enslaved; should the contrary happen, it shall be null and have no effect.

By virtue of Our apostolic authority We define and declare by these present letters, or by any translation thereof signed by any notary public and sealed with the seal of any ecclesiastical dignitary, which shall thus command the same obedience as the originals, that the said Indians and other peoples should be converted to the faith of Jesus Christ by preaching the word of God and by the example of good and holy living.

[Dated: May 29, 1537]

Chapter 22

People of Esteem:
The Work of Missionaries in China

Letter to Francesco Pasio, SJ, Vice-Provincial of China and Japan

Who Wrote It?

Matteo Ricci was born in Macerata, Italy, in 1552. A few months before his nineteenth birthday, Ricci joined the Society of Jesus, the Jesuit order, and studied mathematics, cosmology, and astronomy. In 1583 he began his mission to China, where he worked for twenty-seven years. He died in Beijing, China, in 1610.

When Was It Written?

Matteo Ricci wrote his letter on February 15, 1609, after twenty-one years of ministry in China.

Why Was It Written?

In his letter to Francesco Pasio, Matteo Ricci requests the continued support of his superior. But the letter also outlines Ricci's method of evangelization. Missionary efforts had been undertaken previously in China, but Ricci was the first missionary to have a significant and lasting impact upon the Church's presence in China. His success was due to his respect for the Chinese culture and his efforts at integrating

Christianity into that culture. Ricci's methods eventually led to the conversion of a quarter-million Christians within 100 years of the beginning of his mission. Even so, Ricci wasn't interested in a particular number of converts; he was more interested in the quality of people's commitment to Christianity.

Why Is It Still Important Today?

Matteo Ricci, because of his method of trying to understand and respect a culture different from his own, is an excellent role model for modern evangelizers. Sadly, his method of adapting Christian practice to the Chinese culture was fiercely challenged by later missionaries. In the early eighteenth century, those missionaries persuaded the Church to formally forbid many of Ricci's adaptations. The end result was the collapse of Christianity in China. In the 1930s, Rome reinstated Ricci's methods. In 2001 Pope John Paul II spoke of the Church's efforts in China following Ricci's presence there:

> I feel deep sadness for these errors and limits of the past, and I regret that in many people these failings may have given the impression of a lack of respect and esteem for the Chinese people on the part of the Catholic Church, making them feel that the Church was motivated by feelings of hostility towards China. For all of this I ask the forgiveness and understanding of those who may have felt hurt in some way by such actions on the part of Christians.

Ricci understood that Christ's good news could be communicated in a way that sounded like good news to the Chinese. His example and methods anticipated the approach to evangelization that would be adopted by the Second Vatican Council.

Primary Source: Letter to Francesco Pasio, SJ, Vice-Provincial of China and Japan

Seeing that many weighty persons actually deal with us and have very great esteem for the integrity of our lives, they fear that they might be reproved especially since we are foreigners—to whom the Chinese never want to be discourteous. What is more, they think that the emperor holds us in high regard. If they were to issue a memorandum against us without the emperor taking any action, it would redound to their shame and confusion. And finally, granted that they cannot find any evil great enough to merit punishment in our lives, and since it does not seem appropriate to them for us to be exiled, which would cause us to think scandalously of China, they let us live in peace. Not finding a better occasion against us which we will certainly avoid giving them, I think they will not take action against us until a much later date. I think this is what I was referring to previously in regard to asking for permission for our priests to remain in China and of both the dangers and security that I think we now have.

As to this feeling of security I could go on at great length for I have the greatest hope of immense progress for the Church in this immense country. Thus I will only touch briefly on a few points in order not to make this letter too lengthy.

A first reason for this hope is a consideration of the beginning and progress of this mission which has been rather miraculous, and similar to other divine manifestations, although ever accompanied by many sufferings and conflicts which continue even today. Despite these drawbacks we continue to grow daily in reputation, in numbers, and in quality of the converts, as your Excellency surety has noticed in past reports and from current reports. Since our converts already number in the thousands, and in both courts and in the other two major cities we now enjoy the greatest reputation that we have ever had. Mingling with the top men of the realm we are considered not only very virtuous men but also learned men of some great stature, two characteristics that are greatly esteemed here.

Secondly, because in China intellectual activity is highly prized or looked up to as science and opinion based on reason, there is really no other nobility which is recognized here except of the academic life and of those who achieve eminence and degrees in it. Since this is so, I think it will be easy to persuade the elite of the kingdom of the truths or our holy faith which are confirmed with so much reasonable evidence. For if the intelligentsia agrees with us, it will be far easier to convert the masses.

The third reason which naturally follows is the facility we have in spreading our holy Christian religion through books which we procure from all parts of the world without any difficulty. For books are so easily circulated and reach more people and express matters more clearly and more precisely than is possible by word of mouth, which we have already experienced here in China. In fact our holy religion and its good reputation have been spread much more through the four or five books which have been published up to now than was ever done before through words or other means of ours. As a matter of fact, without those books I realized that they considered our holy religion much different than what it is actually. And this exceptional help exists in this nation but not in any of the other oriental lands. I can promise your Excellency that if we can transmit exactly by means of books all the truths of our holy faith, the Chinese will be able to spread the Christian religion by themselves with very little additional instruction. They would maintain themselves as solid Christians even though, it should happen that for some reason our priests could no longer be among them.

Fourthly, the Chinese have a marvelous and sharp natural intelligence. This is immediately evident in their books, their speeches and in their clothing of such artistry, and in the intricacies of their government which is the marvel of the entire Orient. Furthermore, if we could teach them our sciences, not only would they succeed as very eminent men, but through them we could also easily lead them to our holy faith. Indeed they would never forget such a great favor of which even today we have manifest signs. For although up to now we have only taught them a little of the mathematical sciences and of cosmography, still they feel so indebted towards us that many times I have heard with my own ears from important people that we have indeed opened the eyes of the Chinese who were previously blind. This they have said only of the natural sciences. What will they say then of the more obscure and theoretical sciences such as physics, metaphysics, theology and the supernatural sciences?

Fifthly, although the contrary might seem true to others, they are also inclined toward piety. I have come to be convinced of this gradually through the years. If we go back to their earliest history we see that they followed the natural law much more faithfully than did Europeans. Fifteen hundred years ago these people were little given to the worship of idols. Those idols that they did adore were not so evil as the ones the Egyptians, Greeks, and Romans worshiped. They were rather beings that they considered very virtuous and of whom they narrated very good deeds. Actually the books of the intellectuals which are the most ancient and the most authoritative give adoration only to the heavens, and the earth, and the emperor of these. Examining thoroughly all these books, we will find in them very few points which are against human reason and indeed many things conformable to it, without yielding completely to any of their natural philosophers. We can even hope that with divine mercy many of these ancients even saved their souls by observing the natural law with some help that God in his goodness might have given them. After the spread of the idols in this country, we should not pay so much attention to the slender recognition that the Chinese paid to these idols (some gave none at all). We should rather praise them for having recognized that these idols were not solidly founded and worthy of esteem, and therefore they refused to give them more honor than they really deserved. We can therefore hope that the contrary will be true in their attitude towards the Catholic faith. However, the attention that they pay to the idols is not so insignificant that their cities inside and outside of the walls are not dotted with many, ornate, and sumptuous temples which are staffed by thousands of ministers whom they support by the revenue of the temple itself or by alms. These gods are well constructed in wood or bronze or in other materials, and they are shown much veneration by women and the common people so that these pagan people in their homes externally even seem to surpass the worship that the Christians show to the true God.

Chapter 23

Money, Workers, and Fairness:
Catholic Social Teaching Begins

Rerum Novarum

Who Wrote It?

On February 20, 1878, Pope Leo XIII was elected the 256th successor of Saint Peter as the leader of the Church. He died on July 20, 1903, after making many contributions to the welfare of the Church and to the peoples of the world.

When Was It Written?

Rerum Novarum was issued as a papal encyclical letter on May 15, 1891.

Encyclical Letter

An encyclical letter is a teaching document written by a pope. Among the many different writings a pope produces—such as apostolic exhortations, apostolic constitutions, messages, and homilies—encyclical letters are the most authoritative.

Why Was It Written?

Pope Leo XIII was particularly concerned about the dehumanizing effects that the industrial revolution and the intellectual movement called the Enlightenment were having on the working class. He believed that both Marxism and unbridled capitalism victimized workers. He argued for the establishment of just wages, with the needs of the workers in mind, and called for a greater concern for the common good of the community as opposed to the absolute rights of the individual. At the same time, he cautioned the world against the evils in any overzealous theory of socialism that seemed to promote conflict between social classes.

Why Is It Still Important Today?

Today's social teaching finds its roots in *Rerum Novarum,* which has become the cornerstone of that teaching. *Rerum Novearum* has been echoed and expanded upon by most of the Popes who followed Pope Leo XIII, including John XXIII, Paul VI, and John Paul II. The importance of this monumental encyclical has endured because, sadly, many dehumanizing conditions have also endured. *Rerum Novarum* reminds Catholics that they are always advocates for those who are poor and for the working class. Catholics are also transformative agents of change for a more just society.

Primary Source: *Rerum Novarum*

That the spirit of revolutionary change, which has long been disturbing the nations of the world, should have passed beyond the sphere of politics and made its influence felt in the cognate sphere of practical economics is not surprising. The elements of the conflict now raging are unmistakable, in the vast expansion of industrial pursuits and the marvellous discoveries of science; in the changed relations between masters and workmen; in the enormous fortunes of some few individuals, and the utter poverty of the masses; the increased self reliance and closer mutual combination of the working classes; as also, finally, in the prevailing moral degeneracy. The momentous gravity of the state of things now obtaining fills every mind with painful apprehension; wise men are discussing it; practical men are proposing schemes; popular meetings, legislatures, and rulers of nations are all busied with it—actually there is no question which has taken deeper hold on the public mind.

2. Therefore, venerable brethren, as on former occasions when it seemed opportune to refute false teaching, We have addressed you in the interests of the Church and of the common weal, and have issued letters bearing on political power, human liberty, the Christian constitution of the State, and like matters, so have We thought it expedient

now to speak on the condition of the working classes. (1) It is a subject on which We have already touched more than once, incidentally. But in the present letter, the responsibility of the apostolic office urges Us to treat the question of set purpose and in detail, in order that no misapprehension may exist as to the principles which truth and justice dictate for its settlement. The discussion is not easy, nor is it void of danger. It is no easy matter to define the relative rights and mutual duties of the rich and of the poor, of capital and of labor. And the danger lies in this, that crafty agitators are intent on making use of these differences of opinion to pervert men's judgments and to stir up the people to revolt. . . .

4. To remedy these wrongs the socialists, working on the poor man's envy of the rich, are striving to do away with private property, and contend that individual possessions should become the common property of all, to be administered by the State or by municipal bodies. They hold that by thus transferring property from private individuals to the community, the present mischievous state of things will be set to rights, inasmuch as each citizen will then get his fair share of whatever there is to enjoy. But their contentions are so clearly powerless to end the controversy that were they carried into effect the working man himself would be among the first to suffer. They are, moreover, emphatically unjust, for they would rob the lawful possessor, distort the functions of the State, and create utter confusion in the community. . . .

The contention, then, that the civil government should at its option intrude into and exercise intimate control over the family and the household is a great and pernicious error. True, if a family finds itself in exceeding distress, utterly deprived of the counsel of friends, and without any prospect of extricating itself, it is right that extreme necessity be met by public aid, since each family is a part of the commonwealth. In like manner, if within the precincts of the household there occur grave disturbance of mutual rights, public authority should intervene to force each party to yield to the other its proper due; for this is not to deprive citizens of their rights, but justly and properly to safeguard and strengthen them. But the rulers of the commonwealth must go no further; here, nature bids them stop. Paternal authority can be neither abolished nor absorbed by the State; for it has the same source as human life itself. "The child belongs to the father," and is, as it were, the continuation of the father's personality; and speaking strictly, the child takes its place in civil society, not of its own right, but in its quality as member of the family in which it is born. And for the very reason that "the child belongs to the father" it is, as St. Thomas Aquinas says, "before it attains the use of free will, under the power and the charge of its parents." The socialists, therefore, in setting aside the parent and setting up a State supervision, act against natural justice, and destroy the structure of the home. . . .

The great mistake made in regard to the matter now under consideration is to take up with the notion that class is naturally hostile to class, and that the wealthy and the working men are intended by nature to live in mutual conflict. So irrational and so false is this view that the direct contrary is the truth. Just as the symmetry of the human frame is the result of the suitable arrangement of the different parts of the body, so in a State is it ordained by nature that these two classes should dwell in harmony and agreement, so as to maintain the balance of the body politic. Each needs the other: capital cannot do without labor, nor labor without capital. Mutual agreement results in the beauty of good order, while perpetual conflict necessarily produces confusion and savage barbarity. Now, in preventing such strife as this, and in uprooting it, the efficacy of Christian institutions is marvellous and manifold. First of all, there is no intermediary more powerful than religion (whereof the Church is the interpreter and guardian) in drawing the rich and the working class together, by reminding each of its duties to the other, and especially of the obligations of justice. . . .

But the Church, with Jesus Christ as her Master and Guide, aims higher still. She lays down precepts yet more perfect, and tries to bind class to class in friendliness and good feeling. The things of earth cannot be understood or valued aright without taking into consideration the life to come, the life that will know no death. Exclude the idea of futurity, and forthwith the very notion of what is good and right would perish; nay, the whole scheme of the universe would become a dark and unfathomable mystery. The great truth which we learn from nature herself is also the grand Christian dogma on which religion rests as on its foundation—that, when we have given up this present life, then shall we really begin to live. God has not created us for the perishable and transitory things of earth, but for things heavenly and everlasting; He has given us this world as a place of exile, and not as our abiding place. As for riches and the other things which men call good and desirable, whether we have them in abundance, or are lacking in them—so far as eternal happiness is concerned—it makes no difference; the only important thing is to use them aright. Jesus Christ, when He redeemed us with plentiful redemption, took not away the pains and sorrows which in such large proportion are woven together in the web of our mortal life. He transformed them into motives of virtue and occasions of merit; and no man can hope for eternal reward unless he follow in the blood-stained footprints of his Saviour. "If we suffer with Him, we shall also reign with Him." (7) Christ's labors and sufferings, accepted of His own free will, have marvellously sweetened all suffering and all labor. And not only by His example, but by His grace and by the hope held forth of everlasting recompense, has He made pain and grief more easy to endure; "for that which is at present momentary and light of our tribulation, worketh for us above measure exceedingly an eternal weight of glory." (8). . . .

. . . We may lay it down as a general and lasting law that working men's associations should be so organized and governed as to furnish the best and most suitable means for attaining what is aimed at, that is to say, for helping each individual member to better his condition to the utmost in body, soul, and property. It is clear that they must pay special and chief attention to the duties of religion and morality, and that social betterment should have this chiefly in view; otherwise they would lose wholly their special character, and end by becoming little better than those societies which take no account whatever of religion. What advantage can it be to a working man to obtain by means of a society material well-being, if he endangers his soul for lack of spiritual food? "What doth it profit a man, if he gain the whole world and suffer the loss of his soul?" (39) This, as our Lord teaches, is the mark or character that distinguishes the Christian from the heathen. "After all these things do the heathen seek . . . Seek ye first the Kingdom of God and His justice: and all these things shall be added unto you." Let our associations, then, look first and before all things to God; let religious instruction have therein the foremost place, each one being carefully taught what is his duty to God, what he has to believe, what to hope for, and how he is to work out his salvation; and let all be warned and strengthened with special care against wrong principles and false teaching. Let the working man be urged and led to the worship of God, to the earnest practice of religion, and, among other things, to the keeping holy of Sundays and holy days. Let him learn to reverence and love holy Church, the common Mother of us all; and hence to obey the precepts of the Church, and to frequent the sacraments, since they are the means ordained by God for obtaining forgiveness of sin and for leading a holy life. . . .

On each of you, venerable brethren, and on your clergy and people, as an earnest of God's mercy and a mark of Our affection, we lovingly in the Lord bestow the apostolic benediction.

Given at St. Peter's in Rome, the fifteenth day of May, 1891, the fourteenth year of Our pontificate.

Chapter 24

The Vicar of Christ: The First Vatican Council Defines Papal Authority

Pastor Æternus

Who Wrote It?

On June 14, 1846, Pope Blessed Pius IX was elected the 255th successor to Saint Peter, the Vicar of Christ. He was born in Sinigaglia, Italy, in 1792 and died in 1878.

When Was It Written?

Pastor Æternus was written on July 18, 1870, as part of the First Vatican Council. This council was convened in December 1869 and, although the council was never officially closed, the last session was adjourned on September 1, 1870.

Why Was It Written?

When Pope Blessed Pius IX became the Pope in 1846, significant cultural changes were occurring in the world. Pius IX saw many of those changes as threats to the Church and to Christian society. In *Syllabus of Errors,* Pius IX identified and condemned some of the ideological and social developments of the day, including rationalism, communism, naturalism, and interfaith marriages.

Pius IX convened the First Vatican Council to strengthen the power and authority of the Papacy in the face of those threats. That power is most clearly established in *Pastor Æternus,* or *The First Dogmatic Constitution on the Church of Christ,* which declares that the Pope speaks infallibly "in defining doctrine concerning faith or morals."

Why Is It Still Important Today?

The issue of infallibility causes a great deal of confusion among both Catholics and non-Catholics today. Most Christian churches, Catholic and otherwise, accept the teaching that the Church as a whole is infallible when it speaks the truth of Christ, as the Body of Christ, aided by the Holy Spirit.

The confusion arises over the issue of *papal* infallibility as defined at the First Vatican Council. Some have argued against the teaching of the First Vatican Council, claiming that the Pope cannot, on his own, declare a teaching to be infallible. Others have argued that *every* pronouncement made by the Pope should be considered infallible. Neither side prevailed at the First Vatican Council, however. The Pope speaks infallibly when several conditions are met, and only when those conditions are met. For example, the Pope can only speak infallibly on matters of faith and morals. So far, such infallible declarations have only happened twice. In 1854, Pope Pius IX declared infallibly that Mary, the mother of Jesus, was conceived without Original Sin. And, in 1950, Pope Pius XII declared the dogma of the Assumption of Mary to be infallible.

Primary Source: *Pastor Æternus*

Pius, bishop, servant of the servants of God, with the approval of the Sacred Council, for an everlasting record. The eternal shepherd and guardian of our souls, in order to render permanent the saving work of redemption, determined to build a Church in which, as in the house of the living God, all the faithful should be linked by the bond of one faith and charity. Therefore, before he was glorified, he besought his Father, not for the apostles only, but also *for those who were to believe in him through their word, that they all might be one as the Son himself and the Father are one.* So then, just as he sent apostles, whom he chose out of the world, even as he had been sent by the Father, in like manner it was his will that in his church there should be shepherds and teachers until the end of time. In order, then, that the episcopal office should be one and undivided and that, by the union of the clergy, the whole multitude of believers should be held together in the unity of faith and communion, he set blessed Peter over the rest of the apostles and instituted in him the permanent principle of both unities and their visible foundation. Upon the strength of this foundation was to be built the eternal temple, and the church whose topmost part reaches heaven was to rise upon the firmness of this foundation. And since the gates of hell trying, if they can, to overthrow the Church, make their assault with a hatred that increases day by day against its divinely laid foundation, we judge it necessary, with the approbation of the sacred council, and for the protection, defence and growth of the catholic flock, to propound the doctrine concerning the institution, permanence and nature of the sacred and apostolic primacy, upon which the strength and coherence of the whole church depends. This doctrine is to be believed and held by all the faithful in accordance with the ancient and unchanging faith of the whole Church. Furthermore, we shall proscribe and condemn the contrary errors which are so harmful to the Lord's flock. . . .

Episcopal Office

The Greek word for a guardian or an overseer is *episcopos*. In this context, "episcopal" refers to the bishop, not to a person of the Episcopal faith.

Anathema

Anathema, the Church's strongest condemnation, literally means to be cursed.

Therefore, if anyone says that blessed Peter the apostle was not appointed by Christ the lord as prince of all the apostles and visible head of the whole church militant; or that it was a primacy of honour only and not one of true and proper jurisdiction that he directly and immediately received from our lord Jesus Christ himself: let him be anathema. . . .

Therefore, if anyone says that it is not by the institution of Christ the lord himself (that is to say, by divine law) that blessed Peter should have perpetual successors in the primacy over the whole church; or that the Roman pontiff is not the successor of blessed Peter in this primacy: let him be anathema. . . .

So, then, if anyone says that the Roman pontiff has merely an office of supervision and guidance, and not the full and supreme power of jurisdiction over the whole church, and this not only in matters of faith and morals, but also in those which concern the discipline and government of the church dispersed throughout the whole world; or that he has only the principal part, but not the absolute fullness, of this supreme power; or that this power of his is not ordinary and immediate both over all and each of the churches and over all and each of the pastors and faithful: let him be anathema.

That apostolic primacy which the Roman pontiff possesses as successor of Peter, the prince of the apostles, includes also the supreme power of teaching. This holy see has always maintained this, the constant custom of the church demonstrates it, and the ecumenical councils, particularly those in which East and West met in the union of faith and charity, have declared it. So the fathers of the fourth Council of Constantinople, following the footsteps of their predecessors, published this solemn profession of faith: The first condition of salvation is to maintain the rule of the true faith. And since that saying of our lord Jesus Christ, *You are Peter, and upon this rock I will build my Church,* cannot fail of its effect, the words spoken are confirmed by their consequences. For in the apostolic see the catholic religion has always been preserved unblemished, and sacred doctrine been held in honour. Since it is our earnest desire to be in no way separated from this faith and doctrine, we hope that we may deserve to remain in that one communion which the apostolic see preaches, for in it is the whole and true strength of the christian religion. What is more, with the approval of the second council of Lyons, the Greeks made the following profession: "The holy Roman church possesses the supreme and full primacy and principality over the whole catholic church. She truly and humbly acknowledges that she received this from the Lord himself in blessed Peter, the prince and chief of the apostles, whose successor the Roman Pontiff is, together with the fullness of power. And since before all others she has the duty of defending the truth of the faith, so if any questions arise concerning the faith, it is by her judgment that they must be settled."

Then there is the definition of the Council of Florence: "The Roman pontiff is the true vicar of Christ, the head of the whole church and the father and teacher of all Christians; and to him was committed in blessed Peter, by our lord Jesus Christ, the full power of tending, ruling and governing the whole church."

To satisfy this pastoral office, our predecessors strove unwearyingly that the saving teaching of Christ should be spread among all the peoples of the world; and with equal care they made sure that it should be kept pure and uncontaminated wherever it was received. It was for this reason that the bishops of the whole world, sometimes individually, sometimes gathered in synods, according to the long established custom of the churches and the pattern of ancient usage, referred to this apostolic see those dangers especially which arose in matters concerning the faith. This was to ensure that any damage suffered by the faith should be repaired in that place above all where the faith can know no failing. The Roman pontiffs, too, as the circumstances of the time or the state of affairs suggested, sometimes by summoning ecumenical councils or consulting the opinion of the churches scattered throughout the world, sometimes by special synods, sometimes by taking advantage of other useful means afforded by divine providence, defined as doctrines to be held those things which, by God's help, they knew to be in keeping with Sacred Scripture and the apostolic traditions. For the Holy Spirit was promised to the successors of Peter not so that they might, by his revelation, make known some new doctrine, but that, by his assistance, they might religiously guard and faithfully expound the revelation or deposit of faith transmitted by the apostles. Indeed, their apostolic teaching was embraced by all the venerable fathers and reverenced and followed by all the holy orthodox doctors, for they knew very well that this see of St. Peter always remains unblemished by any error, in accordance with the divine promise of our Lord and Saviour to the prince of his disciples: *I have prayed for you that your faith may not fail; and when you have turned again, strengthen your brethren.*

This gift of truth and never-failing faith was therefore divinely conferred on Peter and his successors in this see so that they might discharge their exalted office for the salvation of all, and so that the whole flock of Christ might be kept away by them from the poisonous food of error and be nourished with the sustenance of heavenly doctrine. Thus the tendency to schism is removed and the whole church is preserved in unity, and, resting on its foundation, can stand firm against the gates of hell.

But since in this very age when the salutary effectiveness of the apostolic office is most especially needed, not a few are to be found who disparage its authority, we judge it absolutely necessary to affirm solemnly the prerogative which the only-begotten Son of God was pleased to attach to the supreme pastoral office.

Therefore, faithfully adhering to the tradition received from the beginning of the christian faith, to the glory of God our saviour, for the exaltation of the catholic religion and for the salvation of the christian people, with the approval of the sacred council, we teach and define as a divinely revealed dogma that when the Roman pontiff speaks *ex cathedra*, that is, when, in the exercise of his office as shepherd and teacher of all Christians, in virtue of his supreme apostolic authority, he defines a doctrine concerning faith or morals to be held by the whole church, he possesses, by the divine assistance promised to him in blessed Peter, that infallibility which the divine Redeemer willed his church to enjoy in defining doctrine concerning faith or morals. Therefore, such definitions of the Roman pontiff are of themselves, and not by the consent of the church, irreformable.

So then, should anyone, which God forbid, have the temerity to reject this definition of ours: let him be anathema.

Chapter 25

Year in the Life:
An Account of Life in the Spanish Colonies

Report on the Mission of San Carlos de Monterey

Who Wrote It?

Fray Junípero Serra was born on the Spanish island of Mallorca in 1713 and died in California in 1784. At age sixteen, he joined the Franciscan order and soon became known for his sharp intellect. Although his keen mind made him a worthy professor at age twenty-four, it also made him restless. Serra wanted something more.

He sought and was granted permission to go to Mexico City, Mexico, to work in the Spanish colonies in the New World. He eventually came to what is modern-day California and worked to establish missions and to convert the native peoples to Christianity. Because of his work founding communities in the colony, a statue of Serra stands in the U.S. Capitol to commemorate his significance to Californian and American history.

When Was It Written?

Fray Junípero Serra wrote his report on July 1, 1784.

Why Was It Written?

This document is, in a sense, Fray Junípero Serra's will. As a Franciscan, he was committed to the values of poverty established by Saint Francis.

Therefore, he had no material goods to leave to anyone. But he did have his life's work, and one senses he was bequeathing the fruits of thirty-five years of evangelization to the Church and to his brother Franciscans. Serra died soon after this document was written.

Why Is It Still Important Today?

Fray Junípero Serra's accomplishments, like those of so many missionaries, give us a model of commitment and dedication to spreading the Gospel. At the same time, his work is not without controversy. Some have criticized him for disrupting the culture of the indigenous people of California and for assisting the Spanish government in colonizing the land. Nevertheless, Serra was motivated by his dedication to the Gospel. He easily could have chosen to stay on his native island of Mallorca, where he would have had a comfortable career as a preacher and professor of theology. Instead, he opted for a life of poverty and hardship to bring the Good News to New Spain.

Primary Source:
Report on the Mission of San Carlos de Monterey

Year 1771
Hail Jesus, Mary, Joseph!
On the most solemn feast of the Holy Spirit, Pentecost Sunday, June 3, 1770, this mission of San Carlos de Monterey was founded to the joy of the sea and land expeditions. In a short time the rejoicing was shared by the entire kingdom and eagerly celebrated in both Spains.

On that day, after imploring the assistance of the Holy Spirit, the sacred standard of the cross was blessed, raised, and adored by all. The ground was blessed, an altar set up, and a sort of chapel formed with naval flags. The holy sacrifice of the Mass was sung, a sermon was preached, and, at the end, the *Te Deum* was intoned. With these (ceremonies), possession was duly taken of Monterey for (our) holy Church and

Both Spains

There were two Spains at that time of Fray Junípero Serra. The European country of Spain was one. The other was New Spain, the Spanish colonies in the Americas.

the crown of Spain. A legal document covering all was drawn up and will be found where it belongs. All this occurred on the beach at the landing place of the said port, the same spot on which one hundred sixty-seven years before, as it is written, the expedition of Don Sebastián Vizcaino had celebrated Mass.

Presidio

Presidio refers to a military fort or a secured settlement in a Spanish territory or colony.

The following day, after choosing the most likely spot on that plain, the construction of the presidio was enthusiastically begun by the men of both sea and land forces. By the fourteenth of the same month, the most solemn feast of Corpus (Christi), a chapel had been built, as well as it could be, at the spot in the presidio which it still occupies, and a high Mass was sung with the Blessed Sacrament exposed in its monstrance. After the Mass there was a procession, in which His Sacramental Majesty passed over the ground that till then had been so heathen and miserable. It was a day of great consolation for all of us who were Christians.

So the presidio was begun but the troop was too small to be divided into two bodies. Thus we, the religious, were forced to establish ourselves in and remain incorporated with this presidio until further arrangements [could be made], even though we knew that there we could do no sowing or any other kind of work.

We remained like this for one year, spending the time putting in order our residence and the most necessary storerooms for our supplies and in making friends with the Indians who were coming to see us; and we tried to win some children. In fact, within a short time, we baptized three and when the boat returned at the end of the year [1771], we had already twenty new Christians at Monterey. As ten religious came on this vessel, we were then twelve. We all dressed in rich chasubles and had a most solemn procession for Corpus (Christi). We had here the vestments for future missions, the men from the ship, and those of the land force, etc. Thanks be to God!

In August, 1771, with the express consent of His Excellency, Marquis de Croix, at that time viceroy of New Spain, and of the Illustrious Inspector General, Don José de Gálvez, both of whom officially informed me about this, San Carlos Mission was begun at the site it now occupies on the banks of Carmel River and in view of the sea at the distance of about a cannon shot where it forms the little bay south of Point Pinos. [The mission is] a little more than a league from the royal presidio, which is to the north in latitude 36°44". The next place to the south is San Antonio [Mission], about twenty-five leagues away. Santa Clara [Mission] is in the opposite direction and a little farther away.

On the twenty-fourth of the said month, the feast of St. Bartholomew, the apostle, the holy cross was set up at the site and the first Mass celebrated under a temporary arbor. For four months only one father stayed here with the personnel doing the building. The other priest with the two missionaries destined for the future San Luis [Obispo] Mission remained at the presidio until Christmas Eve that same year. After previously transferring everything belonging to the mission, we left the presidio on foot and arrived here with an escort of eight men: four soldiers, one muleteer, and three servants [who had been] sailors. When we received our share of the stock, after the division, there were great and small eighteen head of cattle; namely, nine cows, one bull, two heifers, and six small calves. That is all the cattle of that which the mission has and all which the mission has spent. I will write further on about the rest.

The eight remaining days of the year were spent in fiestas and in putting things in order.

Year 1783

We can consider this the happiest year of the mission because the number of baptisms was one hundred seventy-five and of marriages thirty-six.

The sowing of all grains amounted to eighty-four bushels, eight pecks. This included one bushel and a half of wheat, half a bushel of corn, and two pecks of beans, which were sown for the [Lower] California Indians, who had moved here and were married in this mission.

And the harvest, less the amount of forty-seven bushels which belonged to these Indians and other concessions made to the people such as a portion of the barley which they might reap and some twenty bushels of wheat from the chaff of the threshing, which was stored in the mission granaries amounted to twenty-six hundred fourteen and a half bushels, that is, of measured barley six hundred seventy bushels, eight hundred thirty-five of wheat, only two hundred according to our estimate are kept in the ear. There were nine hundred seventy-one bushels of corn of both kinds according to our estimate, sixty-three bushels of peas, sixteen bushels of horse beans, four bushels of lentils, and fifty-three bushels of various kinds of beans.

Today the new Christians of this mission number six hundred fourteen living persons, even though some of them take a leave of absence from time to time. They have been maintained and are maintained without any scarcity and we supplied the quartermaster of the presidio of San Carlos with one hundred thirty bushels of Indian corn; because they did not ask for more, also with thirty bushels of beans. The escort of this mission, at the request of the ensign quartermaster, received rations in these two kinds of grain. There have not been other deliveries of consequence so that in our prudent judgment of the two chief commodities, wheat and corn, about half the amount harvested may still remain.

The value of the food supplied to the presidio has been paid already in cloth, which now covers the Indians who grew the crops, but at that we are still distressed at the sight of so much nudity among them.

We do not get clothing now from the soldiers, as we did formerly, not even from those who have debts to us no matter how small. The wool, which in some of the missions is enough to cover Indian nakedness, here has not been any help to us so far, because the thefts of sheep are so numerous that already for more than three years, we can not exceed two hundred head between goats and sheep, and from shearing the few that we have we get nothing worthwhile.

The condition, then, of the Mission in things spiritual is that up to this day in this Mission:

Baptisms 1,006
Confirmations 936

And since those of the other missions belong in some way to this it is noted in passing that their number is . . . 5,307

Marriages in this mission 259
Burials 356

The number of Christian families living at the mission and eating jointly, as well as widowers, single men, and children of both sexes, is evident from the enclosed census lists and so is omitted here.

They pray twice daily with the priest in the church. More than one hundred twenty of them confess in Spanish and many who have died used to do it as well. The others confess as best they can. They work at all kinds of mission labor, such as farm hands, herdsmen, cowboys, shepherds, milkers, diggers, gardeners, carpenters, farmers, irrigators, reapers, blacksmiths, sacristans, and they do everything else that comes along for their corporal and spiritual welfare.

The work of clearing the fields once, sometimes twice, or even three times a year, is considerable because the land is very fertile. When we clear new land great hardship is required. Altogether there is sufficient land cleared for sowing more than one hundred bushels of wheat, and it is sowed in that grain, barley, vegetables, and corn. Every year we clear a little more.

Varas

A *varas* was a Spanish unit of measure that equaled 2.8 feet.

To the seven months' work required to take water from the river for irrigation, as mentioned above, we must add the labor of bringing it to the lagoon near the mission residence. In some years, this lagoon used to be dry. Now it is always full, making it a great convenience and a delight to the mission. Some salmon have been placed in the pool and so we have it handy.

The timber palisade was inadequate to protect the seed grain because they steal the paling for firewood. So we dug a circular trench many thousands of varas long. This was a two years' labor and withal nothing sufficed to prevent losses every year.

Some of the land which we cleared for farming was not only covered with long tough grasses and thickets but also with great trees, willows, alders, and so forth, and it has been hard work, as we have already noted, but we hope that it will pay off at a profit. We also have a sizable walled garden [which produces] abundant vegetables and some fruit.

Chapter 26

Concern for Souls: A Bishop's Anxiety over the Faith of Slaves in Mississippi

A Letter to the Society for the Propagation of the Faith

Who Wrote It?

William Henry Elder was born in Baltimore, Maryland, in 1819 and was appointed bishop of the Diocese of Natchez, Mississippi, in 1857. In 1880 he was transferred to Cincinnati, Ohio, to serve as an auxiliary bishop in that archdiocese. He eventually became the archbishop of Cincinnati in 1883. After establishing a reputation as a good administrator and a compassionate pastor, Elder died in Cincinnati in 1904.

When Was It Written?

Archbishop William Henry Elder wrote his report to the Society for the Propagation of the Faith in 1858, one year after his appointment as bishop of Natchez. At that time, the state of Mississippi had over 400,000 slaves—more than the 309,878 slaves listed in the 1850 census that Elder cited in his report. The slave population accounted for more than 55 percent of the state's population.

Why Was It Written?

Archbishop William Henry Elder wrote this report to communicate the conditions of his diocese after he had ministered there for a year. He was obviously most distressed by the lack of clergy needed to minister to the slaves of his diocese. He was hoping to receive some support in his ministry from the Society for the Propagation of the Faith.

Why Is It Still Important Today?

This document is a difficult mix of both praiseworthy and troubling attitudes. On one hand, Archbishop William Henry Elder argued that the slaves had dignity and were human beings in need of hearing the good news of salvation. Most people at the time did not share that opinion. On the other hand, Elder made disparaging remarks about the conduct and the intellect of the slaves.

Without excusing the failings of Elder and the Catholic Church in the American South, it helps to understand something of the culture. Both the hierarchy and the white Catholic slaveholders were part of the American South. The economic power of the region was built upon the slave labor of Africans and African-Americans. Slavery was not only an economic issue but also a cultural issue. The dominant Southern view of the time was that a superior culture had emerged from a superior people. Because of this perceived superiority, enslaving others was permissible. Although it seems today that Elder would have been able to break free of those cultural circumstances, he did advocate for the liberation of the souls and argued for their instinctive worth. Through reading this document, an awareness of our own cultural limitations might emerge. We must ask: "Are there attitudes in the present-day society that are contrary to the Gospel as slavery was in the nineteenth century?"

Primary Source:
A Letter to the Society for the Propagation of the Faith

Gentlemen

The business of my Diocese has made it necessary for me to spend much time in travelling. I have now been absent from home nearly two months continually, & in the spring likewise I was nearly two months away. Hence it has been impossible for me to write to you earlier as I had intended; & even now I cannot give you the full & interesting account of our missions which I had hoped to prepare, both from want of time on my own part, & because I have not got reports from the

Pastors on the various points on which I would desire to inform you. Moreover, being obliged even now to write at various times & in various places, without the facilities which I should have at home for rendering my letter into French, you must pardon [me] for simply writing to you in English.

I beg of you to send me a number of copies of the sheet you have printed containing the heads on which you desire information. I have only found one by accident, & not in time to ask of the Pastors information on those points. I shall follow them however & give you the best information at present in my possession.

The Diocese of Natchez comprises the State of Mississippi, & has an area of 47,000 square miles or about 5,400 square leagues.

The *Number* of *Catholics* was stated in the Almanac several years ago, to be about *ten thousand.* I have not been able to learn how that estimate was made, nor how much reliance can be placed upon it. I believe that if all the Catholics could be counted, who are scattered through the interior of the country, the number would be much greater. I hope that next year we shall know more about it.

The whole Population of the State according to the Census taken in 1850 was 606,526. Speaking generally we may say that all of them profess to be Christians. A great many however do not belong to any particular Denomination, & even among those who do, a considerable number have never been baptized. The Baptists expressly reject the practice of baptizing infants, & very few Protestants look upon it as necessary for salvation.

The most prevalent sects are the Methodists and Baptists. Presbyterians are likewise numerous; the Episcopalians or Anglicans are but few, so far as I have learned.

But it is necessary for you to understand that more than half our population consists of *negro slaves,* who number 309,878; besides free negroes to the number of 930.

These poor negroes form in some respects my chief anxiety. I believe they are generally well cared for, so far as health & the necessaries of life are concerned. But for learning & practising religion, they have at present very little opportunity indeed. Commonly their Masters are well disposed to allow them religious instruction, & sometimes they pay Ministers to come & preach on the plantation. They do not like to let the negroes go to a public church, because there is danger of their misbehaving when they are away from home, & out of sight of the Overseer; & because various inconveniences result from the servants of one plantation mingling with those of another. Each master has something particular in his regulations & his method of management, & if the servants have free intercourse together, they are apt to make each other jealous & dissatisfied.

Some masters indeed object to having a Minister come to preach to their slaves, & they rather encourage some one of the blacks themselves to become a preacher for the rest. You may imagine what kind of religious instruction the poor creatures get.

Catholic masters of course are taught that it is their duty to furnish their slaves with opportunities for being well instructed, & for practising their religion. And here is my anxiety, that I cannot enable those masters to do their duty because there are not Priests enough. The negroes must be attended in a great measure on the plantation, both for the reasons given above, & because in our case there are so few churches; & even where there is a church, the negroes of four or five plantations would fill it up, & leave no room for the white, nor for the other negroes of the neighborhood. The Priest then must go to the plantations, & these are scattered at great distances through the country. All the Priests that I have are residing in congregations from which they cannot be absent long. We need a band of travelling Missionaries who should attend to these plantations, & at the same time hunt out the Catholics scattered through the country. In both of these ways an immensity of good can be done. The poor negroes very often have at first a fear of a Catholic Priest, or imagine they can never understand him; but they are not ill disposed towards religion. Indeed they often have a craving for its ministrations. Having few comforts & no expectations in this world, their thoughts & desires are the more easily drawn to the good things of the world to come. I say often because often again they are so entirely animal in their inclinations, so engrossed with the senses, that they have no regard for any thing above the gratifications of the body. But even among such as these, the missionary often finds a good soil for the seed of religion, because their sensuality arises not so much from malice, as from the want of religious instruction—the want of knowing that there is anything better than this world within their reach. It is true, when from this ignorance they have formed habits of sin, they are not always ready to abandon them when better instructed; but patient & persevering instruction & exhortation, together with the use of the Sacraments, will commonly succeed at last in bringing them to a better life.

For the negro is naturally inclined to be dependent on others; therefore he is disposed to listen & believe what he is told by his superiors. When he resists the teachings of religion, it is not so much from stubbornness as from weakness of mind & will. This weakness of mind makes it hard for him to understand an argument; his weakness of will makes it hard to resist temptation, & still harder to break bad habits. It makes him also liable to great fickleness. This is one of the hard trials of a missionary among them. It is not uncommon for a negro to attend religious instruction for a considerable time with great fidelity & a lively interest, & yet drop off before receiving the Sacraments. Sometimes there is no apparent cause, but just fickleness of character, or perhaps secret temptation. But more generally it may be traced to some irregularity in the instruction, or some little neglect which begets an indifference on their part. They are very much creatures of feeling. If they are attended to regularly & if their instructor takes great interest in them, & gets them to realize the value of their souls, he can do a great deal with them for the glory of God. And he may have the unspeakable consolation of finding among them vocations to a high degree of sanctity. The humility of their condition & the docility of their character take away many of the ordinary obstacles to the workings of grace; & where other circumstances are favourable, these lowly ones in the eyes of the world sometimes rise very high in the favour of God. I have known a case of a servant girl's being really revered as a saint by the family in which she had been reared, & where she was working with all simplicity & fidelity in the lowest offices.

Oh! what a harvest of souls among these 310,000 negroes: every one of them immortal, made to the image & likeness of God, redeemed by the Precious Blood of the Son of God! Oh! what a frightful havoc Satan is making among them! What numbers of children die without baptism! how many grown persons live & die in ignorance of God, and still worse, buried in miserable sins & habits of sins, which they neither know nor care to free themselves from. Oh! for a band of Apostles like Fr. Claver, to devote themselves to the service of the negro. Not such service indeed as he rendered to them with so much heroism; for our blacks are not often in that bodily wretchedness which called forth so much of his charity. They need services less repugnant to flesh & blood, & yet not less fruitful in the saving of souls & promoting the glory of God. They need instructions & the Sacraments. The Masters provide for their bodies & even in a great measure for their exterior conduct. Are there not Priests of God—at least in the generous Apostolic land of France—are there not still some there, who are ready to put the sickle into this abundant field? It will cost pains & patience, but the consolations will be very great, as they gather those rich sheaves of more than golden fruit into the granary of heaven.

Saint Peter Claver

Saint Peter Claver was a Jesuit missionary to what is present-day Colombia. From 1610 until he died in 1654, he worked with the African slaves in Colombia. He vowed that he would devote his life to being a slave for the slaves. For this work, he was named among the patron saints of missionaries.

Chapter 27

More Than a Tabloid:
The Power of *The Catholic Worker*

The Long Loneliness

Who Wrote It?

Dorothy Day was born in Brooklyn, New York, in 1897, but at a young age, she moved with her family to San Francisco, California, and then to Chicago, Illinois. Her time in Chicago formed her love for those who were poor. Day wandered through the poor sections of the South Side and found that she yearned to be in solidarity with the people there and to work for their rights. On those streets her love for the underclasses stirred.

Her activism found a voice in socialism and Communism. But she also found that she was attracted to Catholic spirituality. As much as Communism professed to be for the rights of the worker, the ideology opposed religious expression. Eventually, Day became a Catholic, but she was unsure of a way to harmonize her spiritual beliefs and her work as a social activist. She found a way: *The Catholic Worker.* In this simple tabloid, she promoted the Catholic Church's teachings on social justice, and *The Catholic Worker* was an immediate success. In only six months, it grew from 2,500 printed copies per month to 100,000. Day died in 1980 and unarguably left behind the most influential voice for promoting Catholic social teaching.

When Was It Written?

Dorothy Day wrote *The Long Loneliness* in 1952, during a time when important social issues raged. The civil rights movement, the Cold War, and nuclear arms were all pressing topics of the day.

Why Was It Written?

The Long Loneliness is Dorothy Day's story of the founding of *The Catholic Worker* newspaper and the social movement of the same name in 1933. It is also Day's spiritual autobiography. The work provides a vivid account of her growth in faith and her commitment to the Good News proclaimed by Christ to those who are poor. Through this account, she hoped to expand the Church's work and mission toward poor and oppressed people.

Why Is It Still Important Today?

Even before she died in 1980, some people called Dorothy Day an American saint. She resisted that notion because she believed people would stop taking her seriously if they believed she was holier than they were. She was intent on creating, in everyone, a revolution of the heart so that the needy in society would have enough food to eat, a decent place to live, and meaningful work to do. Today more than 140 Catholic Worker communities committed to Catholic social teaching exist. Countless more people have been inspired by Day's selfless commitment to the Gospel. Day's story is important to read because it demonstrates how an ordinary person can follow Christ in a serious and radical way.

Primary Source: *The Long Loneliness*

The Catholic Worker, as the name implied, was directed to the worker, but we used the word in its broadest sense, meaning those who worked with hand or brain, those who did physical, mental or spiritual work. But we thought primarily of the poor, the dispossessed, the exploited.

Every one of us who was attracted to the poor had a sense of guilt, of responsibility, a feeling that in some way we were living on the labor of others. The fact that we were born in a certain environment, were enabled to go to school, were endowed with the ability to compete with others and hold our own, that we had few physical disabilities—all these things marked us as the privileged in a way. We felt a respect for the poor and destitute as those nearest to God, as those chosen by Christ for His compassion. Christ lived among men. The great mystery of the Incarnation, which meant that God became man that man might become God, was a joy that made us want to kiss the earth in worship, because His feet once trod that same earth. It was a mystery that we as Catholics accepted, but there were also the facts of Christ's life, that He was born in a stable, that He did not come to be a temporal King, that He worked with His hands, spent the first years of His life in exile, and the rest of His early manhood in a crude carpenter shop in Nazareth. He fulfilled His religious duties in the synagogue and the temple. He trod the roads in His public life and the first men He called were fishermen, small owners of boats and nets. He was familiar with the migrant worker and the proletariat, and some of His parables dealt with them. He spoke of the living wage, not equal pay for equal work, in the parable of those who came at the first and the eleventh hour.

He died between two thieves because He would not be made an earthly King. He lived in an occupied country for thirty years without starting an underground movement or trying to get out from under a foreign power. His teaching transcended all the wisdom of the scribes and Pharisees, and taught us the most effective means of living in this world while preparing for the next. And He directed His sublime words to the poorest of the poor, to the people who thronged the towns and followed after John the Baptist, who hung around, sick and poverty-stricken at the doors of rich men.

He had set us an example and the poor and destitute were the ones we wished to reach. The poor were the ones who had jobs of a sort, organized or unorganized, and those who were unemployed or on work-relief projects. The destitute were the men and women who came to us in the breadlines and we could do little with them but give what we had of food and clothing. Sin, sickness and death accounted for much of human misery. But aside from this, we did not feel that Christ meant we should remain silent in the face of injustice and accept it even though He said, *"The poor ye shall always have with you."* [Mt 21:11; Mk 14:7; Jn 12:8]

In the first issue of the paper we dealt with Negro labor on the levees in the South, exploited as cheap labor by the War Department. We wrote of women and children in industry and the spread of unemployment. The second issue carried a story of a farmers' strike in the Midwest and the condition of restaurant workers in cities. In the third issue there were stories of textile strikes and child labor in that industry; the next month coal and milk strikes. In the sixth issue of the paper we were already combating anti-Semitism. From then on, although we wanted to make our small eight-page tabloid a local paper, that is, covering the American scene, we could not ignore the issues abroad. They had their repercussions at home. We could not write about these issues without being drawn out on the streets on picket lines, and we found ourselves in 1935 with the Communists picketing the German consulate at the Battery.

It was not the first time we seemed to be collaborators. During the Ohrbach Department Store strike the year before I ran into old friends from the Communist group, but I felt then, and do now, that the fact that Communists made issue of Negro exploitation and labor trouble was no reason why we should stay out of the situation. "The truth is the truth," writes St. Thomas, "and proceeds from the Holy Ghost, no matter from whose lips it comes." . . .

One winter I had a speaking engagement in Kansas and my expenses were paid, which fact enabled me to go to Memphis and Arkansas to visit the Tenant Farmers' Union, which was then and is still headed by a Christian Socialist group. The headquarters were a few rooms in Memphis, where the organizers often slept on the floor because there was no money for rent other than that of the offices. Those days I spent with them I lived on sandwiches and coffee because

The Battery

The *Battery* is a section of New York City located at the southern tip of Manhattan.

Collaborator

At the time when *The Long Loneliness* was written, the United States was in an ideological battle with Communism. *Collaborator* was a term used to describe U.S. citizens who had a working relationship with Communist organizations. Being called a collaborator was a serious accusation.

there was no money to spend on regular meals either. We needed to save money for gas to take us around to the centers where dispossessed sharecroppers and tenant farmers were also camping out, homeless, in railroad stations, schools and churches. They were being evicted wholesale because of the purchase of huge tracts of land by northern insurance agencies. The picture has been shown in *Tobacco Road, In Dubious Battle,* and *Grapes of Wrath*—pictures of such desolation and poverty and in the latter case of such courage that my heart was lifted again to hope and love and admiration that human beings could endure so much and yet have courage to go on and keep their vision of a more human life.

During that trip I saw men, women and children herded into little churches and wayside stations, camped out in tents, their household goods heaped about them, not one settlement but many—farmers with no land to farm, housewives with no homes. They tried with desperate hope to hold onto a pig or some chickens, bags of seed, some little beginnings of a new hold on life. It was a bitter winter and frame houses there are not built to withstand the cold as they are in the north. The people just endure it because the winter is short—accept it as part of the suffering of life.

I saw children ill, one old man dead in bed and not yet buried, mothers weeping with hunger and cold. I saw bullet holes in the frame churches, and their benches and pulpit smashed up and windows broken. Men had been kidnapped and beaten; men had been shot and wounded. The month after I left, one of the organizers was killed by a member of a masked band of vigilantes who were fighting the Tenant Farmers' Union.

There was so little one could do—empty one's pockets, give what one had, live on sandwiches with the organizers, and write, write to arouse the public conscience. I telegraphed Eleanor Roosevelt and she responded at once with an appeal to the governor for an investigation. The papers were full of the effrontery of a northern Catholic social worker, as they called me, who dared to pay a four-day visit and pass judgment on the economic situation of the state. The governor visited some of the encampments, and sarcastic remarks were made in some of the newspaper accounts about the pigs and chicken. "If they are starving, let them eat their stock," they wrote. . . .

Yes, we have lived with the poor, with the workers, and we know them not just from the streets, or in mass meetings, but from years of living in the slums, in tenements, in our hospices in Washington, Baltimore, Philadelphia, Harrisburg, Pittsburgh, New York, Rochester, Boston, Worcester, Buffalo, Troy, Detroit, Cleveland, Toledo, Akron, St. Louis, Chicago, Milwaukee, Minneapolis, Seattle, San Francisco, Los Angeles, Oakland, even down into Houma, Louisiana, where Father Jerome Drolet worked with Negroes and whites, with shrimp shellers, fishermen, longshoremen and seamen.

Just as the Church has gone out through its missionaries into the most obscure towns and villages, we have gone too. Sometimes our contacts have been through the Church and sometimes through readers of our paper, through union organizers or those who needed to be organized.

We have lived with the unemployed, the sick, the unemployables. The contrast between the worker who is organized and has his union, the fellowship of his own trade to give him strength, and those who have no organization and come in to us on a breadline is pitiable.

They are stripped then, not only of all earthly goods, but of spiritual goods, their sense of human dignity. When they are forced into line at municipal lodging houses, in clinics, in our houses of hospitality, they are then the truly destitute. Over and over again in our work, many young men and women who came as volunteers have not been able to endure it and have gone away. To think that we are forced by our own lack of room, our lack of funds, to perpetuate this shame, is heartbreaking. . . .

We published many heavy articles on capital and labor, on strikes and labor conditions, on the assembly line and all the other evils of industrialism. But it was a whole picture we were presenting of man and his destiny and so we emphasized less, as the years went by, the organized-labor aspect of the paper.

It has been said that it was *The Catholic Worker* and its stories of poverty and exploitation that aroused the priests to start labor schools, go out on picket lines, take sides in strikes with the worker, and that brought about an emphasis on the need to study sociology in the seminaries.

And many a priest who afterward became famous for his interest in labor felt that we had in a way deserted the field, had left the cause of the union man. Bishops and priests appearing on the platform of the A. F. of L. and C. I. O. conventions felt that we had departed from our original intention and undertaken work in the philosophical and theological fields that might better have been left to the clergy. The discussion of the morality of modern war, for instance, and application of moral principle in specific conflicts. Labor leaders themselves felt that in our judgment of war, we judged them also for working in the gigantic armaments race, as indeed we did. Ours is indeed an unpopular front.

AFL and CIO

The American Federation of Labor (AFL) and the Congress of Industrial Organization (CIO) have historically been the most influential labor unions in the United States and have fought for many of the same rights for which Dorothy Day fought. The two organizations merged to form the AFL-CIO in 1955.

Chapter 28

Traitor to the State, Herald of the Gospel

Letters from a Nazi Prison

Who Wrote It?

Franz Jägerstätter, like many Catholic heroes, did not show early indications of a passionate commitment to the Gospel. He had a reputation for being a rather wild young man. But this changed when he married his wife, Franziska. Jägerstätter became active in his local parish and went to Mass daily. He was building a good, yet quiet, life with Franziska and his three children. He operated their small Austrian farm in the 1930s. But that quiet life would soon change as the Nazi party stretched its influence into his native Austria.

In 1938, when the Nazis took full control of Austria, Jägerstätter refused to cooperate with the new order. He was so committed to the Resistance that he even refused government emergency aid when a storm destroyed his crops. When the Nazis began drafting Austrian men into the army of the Third Reich, Jägerstätter refused to serve. His refusal led to his arrest and eventual execution.

When Was It Written?

Franz Jägerstätter wrote these letters in 1943 in the waning years of World War II, a time when millions of people lost their lives at the hands of Nazi persecutors.

Why Was It Written?

Franz Jägerstätter's writings from prison established his reasons for defying the Nazis. At least three priests and his bishop counseled Jägerstätter to accept service in the German army as a lesser evil than that of leaving his wife and children without a husband and father. In these letters, Jägerstätter provides the reason for his respectful rejection of their counsel. He expresses his belief that his obedience to God required him to resist the evil of the Nazi regime.

Why Is It Still Important Today?

On what would have been Franz Jägerstätter's eightieth birthday, Bishop Thomas J. Gumbleton of Detroit, Michigan, was invited to celebrate Mass in Jägerstätter's village of Saint Radegund, Austria. On that occasion, Gumbleton noted that Jägerstätter "gave up his life in resistance to sin in the public order." He did not die trying to save another person nor working as a missionary in a foreign and hostile land. He died because he took a stand against a sinful society. Many of today's public and social sins are, perhaps, less monstrous. They are sins, nonetheless. By its very nature, sin eventually leads to oppression and misery. Jägerstätter's story offers courage for active resistance to present-day evil.

Primary Source: Letters from a Nazi Prison

"Commentaries" (July 1943)
Is There Anything the Individual Can Still Do?

Today one can hear it said repeatedly that there is nothing any more that an individual can do. If someone were to speak out, it would mean only imprisonment and death. True, there is not much that can be done any more to change the course of world events. I believe that should have begun a hundred or even more years ago. But as long as we live in this world, I believe it is never too late to save ourselves and perhaps some other soul for Christ. One really has no cause to be astonished that there are those who can no longer find their way in the great confusion of our day. People we think we can trust, who ought to be leading the way and setting a good example, are running along with the crowd. No one gives enlightenment, whether in word or in writing.

Or, to be more exact, it may not be given. And the thoughtless race goes on, always closer to eternity. As long as conditions are still half good, we don't see things quite right, or that we could or do otherwise.

But, alas, once hardship and misery break over us, then it will come to us as with the light of day whether everything the crowd does is so right and good, and then for many the end will pass over into despair.

I realize, too, that today many words would accomplish little more than make one highly eligible for prison. Yet, in spite of this, it is not good if our spiritual leaders remain silent year after year. By "words" I mean, of course, instruction; but example gives direction. Do we no longer want to see Christians who are able to take a stand in the darkness around us in deliberate clarity, calmness, and confidence—who, in the midst of tension, gloom, selfishness, and hate, stand fast in perfect peace and cheerfulness—who are not like the floating reed which is driven here and there by every breeze—who do not merely watch to see what their friends will do but, instead, ask themselves, "What does our faith teach us about this," or "can my conscience bear this so easily that I will never have to repent?"

If road signs were ever stuck so loosely in the earth that every wind could break them off or blow them about, would anyone who did not know the road be able to find his way? And how much worse it is if those to whom one turns for information refuse to give him an answer or, at most, give him the wrong direction just to be rid of him as quickly as possible!

Farewell to His Family (August 1943)

All my dear ones, the hour comes ever closer when I will be giving my soul back to God, the Master. I would have liked to say so many things to you in farewell so that it is hard not to be able to take leave of you any more. I would have liked, too, to spare you the pain and sorrow that you must bear because of me. But you know we must love God even more than family, and we must lose everything dear and worthwhile on earth rather than commit even the slightest offense against God. And if, for your sake, I had not shrunk back from offending God, how can we know what sufferings God might have sent us on my account? It must surely have been hard for our dear Savior to bring such pain upon His dear Mother through His death: what, then, are our sorrows compared with what these two innocent hearts had to suffer—and all on account of us sinners?

And what kind of a leave-taking must it be for those who only halfway believe in an eternal life and, consequently, no longer have much hope of a reunion? If I did not have faith in God's mercy, that He would forgive me all my sins, I could scarcely have endured life in a lonely prison with such calm. Moreover, though people charge me with a crime and have condemned me to death as a criminal, I take comfort in the knowledge that not everything which this world considers a crime is a crime in the eyes of God. And I have hope that I need not fear the eternal Judge because of this crime.

Still this sentence of death should serve as a warning. For the Lord God will not deal much differently with us if we think we do not have to obey everything He commands us through His Church to believe and to do. Except that the eternal Judge will not only condemn us to mortal death but to everlasting death as well. For this reason, I have nothing pressing upon my heart more urgently than to make the firm decision to keep all the commandments and to avoid every sin. You must love God, your Lord, and your neighbor as yourself. On these two commandments rests the whole law. Keep these and we can look forward to an early reunion in heaven. For this reason, too, we must not think evil of others who act differently than I. It is much better to pray for everyone than to pass judgment upon them, for God desires that all become blessed.

Many actually believe quite simply that things have to be the way they are. If this should happen to mean that they are obliged to commit injustice, then they believe that others are responsible. The [military] oath would not be a lie for someone who believes he can go along and is willing to do so. But if I know in advance that I cannot accept and obey everything I would promise under that oath, then I would be guilty of a lie. For this reason I am convinced that it is still best that I speak the truth, even if it costs me my life. For you will not find it written in any of the commandments of God or of the Church that a man is obliged under pain of sin to take an oath committing him to obey whatever might be commanded of him by his secular ruler. Therefore, you should not be heavy of heart if others see my decision as a sin, as some already have.

In the same way, if someone argues from the standpoint of the family, do not be troubled, for it is not permitted to lie even for the sake of the family. If I had ten children, the greatest demand upon me would still be the one I must make of myself.

Educate the children to be pious Catholics as long as it is possible. (Now, of course, one cannot expect them to understand much.) I can say from my own experience how painful life is when we live like halfway Christians, that is more like vegetating than living.

If a man were to possess all the wisdom of the world and call half the earth his own, he still could not and would not be as happy as one of those men who can still call virtually nothing in this world their own except their Catholic faith. I would not exchange my lonely cell—which is not at all bad [next word illegible]—for the most magnificent royal palace. No matter how great and how beautiful it might be, it will pass away, but God's word remains for all eternity. I can assure you that if you pray a single sincere "Our Father" for our children, you will have given them a greater gift than if you had provided them with the most lavish dowry a landholder ever dreamed of giving his daughter. Many people would laugh at these words, but they are true just the same.

Now, my dear children, when Mother reads this letter to you, your father will already be dead. He would have loved to come to you again, but the Heavenly Father willed it otherwise. Be good and obedient children and pray for me so that we may soon be reunited in heaven.

Dear wife, forgive me everything by which I have grieved or offended you. For my part, I have forgiven everything. Ask all those in Radegund whom I have ever injured or offended to forgive me too.

Chapter 29

Reading the Signs of the Times:
The Church in the Modern World

Gaudium et Spes

Who Wrote It?

On January 25, 1959, Pope John XXIII announced that he would convene the Church's twenty-first ecumenical council: the Second Vatican Council. After months and years of preparation, the Council opened on October 11, 1962. When the Council ended on December 8, 1965, sixteen major documents had been produced. *Gaudium et Spes*, classified as a constitution, was one of the four major documents.

When Was It Written?

Ecumenical Council

An ecumenical council is the gathering of bishops and theologians from around the world for the purpose of defining Catholic doctrine or of voicing the Church's position on or approach to a particular matter.

Gaudium et Spes was formally issued on December 7, 1965, the day before the Second Vatican Council ended. However, the first idea for the constitution dated to the earliest days of the Council. Cardinal Léon-Joseph Suenens requested that the Council have some foundational principles to guide its work in the years to come. The central vision of the Second Vatican Council is expressed in *Gaudium et Spes*.

Why Was It Written?

Gaudium et Spes is one of the most important documents to come out of the Second Vatican Council. It is a culminating point in a long line of the Church's role in the modern world that began with *Rerum Novarum*. The document provides a set of principles on how the Church should interact with all people to help bring joy and hope to all of humanity. *Gaudium et Spes* was a particularly important statement at a time when some thought the Church should stand apart from society as a way of calling the world to more Christlike values. But the vast majority of bishops at the Council recognized that the Church, and particularly the laity, needed to be deeply involved in the world in order to transform it.

Constitution

Of the sixteen documents that came out of the Second Vatican Council, four have been classified as "constitutions." These documents hold the most weight and are the most authoritative. Two other classifications of documents were issued at the Second Vatican Council: decrees and declarations.

Why Is It Still Important Today?

Pope John Paul II, then Cardinal Karol Józef Wojtyła, was on the commission that drafted *Gaudium et Spes* at the Second Vatican Council; some have observed that a major part of his pontificate has been based on the Church's call as found in that document. In 1980, he said, "It is not difficult to see that in the modern world the sense of justice has been awakening on a vast scale. . . . The Church shares with the people of our time this profound and ardent desire for a life that is just in every aspect, nor does she fail to examine the various aspects of the sort of justice that the life of people and society demands. This is confirmed by the field of Catholic social doctrine" (*Dives in misericordia*, 12).

Gaudium et Spes is the cornerstone of Catholic social doctrine, which teaches us how to strive for justice in today's world. *Gaudium et Spes* is important to read today for the same reason it was important to write in 1965. The Church shares the joys and the hopes of the world. She shares the griefs and the anxieties as well, in solidarity with all those who are afflicted. By following the principles in *Gaudium et Spes*, Christians will be better able to read the signs of the times and act as Jesus would—out of faith and love for all of humanity.

Primary Source: *Gaudium et Spes*

1. The joys and the hopes, the griefs and the anxieties of the men of this age, especially those who are poor or in any way afflicted, these are the joys and hopes, the griefs and anxieties of the followers of Christ. Indeed, nothing genuinely human fails to raise an echo in their hearts. For theirs is a community composed of men. United in Christ, they are led by the Holy Spirit in their journey to the Kingdom of their Father and they have welcomed the news of salvation which is meant for every man. That is why this community realizes that it is truly linked with mankind and its history by the deepest of bonds. . . .

3. Though mankind is stricken with wonder at its own discoveries and its power, it often raises anxious questions about the current trend of the world, about the place and role of man in the universe, about the meaning of its individual and collective strivings, and about the ultimate destiny of reality and of humanity. Hence, giving witness and voice to the faith of the whole people of God gathered together by Christ, this council can provide no more eloquent proof of its solidarity with, a, well as its respect and love for the entire human family with which it is bound up, than by engaging with it in conversation about these various problems. The council brings to mankind light kindled from the Gospel, and puts at its disposal those saving resources which the Church herself, under the guidance of the Holy Spirit, receives from her Founder. For the human person deserves to be preserved; human society deserves to be renewed. Hence the focal point of our total presentation will be man himself, whole and entire, body and soul, heart and conscience, mind and will.

Therefore, this sacred synod, proclaiming the noble destiny of man and championing the Godlike seed which has been sown in him, offers to mankind the honest assistance of the Church in fostering that brotherhood of all men which corresponds to this destiny of theirs. Inspired by no earthly ambition, the Church seeks but a solitary goal: to carry forward the work of Christ under the lead of the befriending Spirit. And Christ entered this world to give witness to the truth, to rescue and not to sit in judgment, to serve and not to be served(2). . . .

4. To carry out such a task, the Church has always had the duty of scrutinizing the signs of the times and of interpreting them in the light of the Gospel. Thus, in language intelligible to each generation, she can

respond to the perennial questions which men ask about this present life and the life to come, and about the relationship of the one to the other. We must therefore recognize and understand the world in which we live, its explanations, its longings, and its often dramatic characteristics. Some of the main features of the modern world can be sketched as follows. . . .

7. A change in attitudes and in human structures frequently calls accepted values into question, especially among young people, who have grown impatient on more than one occasion, and indeed become rebels in their distress. Aware of their own influence in the life of society, they want a part in it sooner. This frequently causes parents and educators to experience greater difficulties day by day in discharging their tasks. The institutions, laws and modes of thinking and feeling as handed down from previous generations do not always seem to be well adapted to the contemporary state of affairs; hence arises an upheaval in the manner and even the norms of behavior.

Finally, these new conditions have their impact on religion. On the one hand a more critical ability to distinguish religion from a magical view of the world and from the superstitions which still circulate purifies it and exacts day by day a more personal and explicit adherence to faith. As a result many persons are achieving a more vivid sense of God. On the other hand, growing numbers of people are abandoning religion in practice. Unlike former days, the denial of God or of religion, or the abandonment of them, are no longer unusual and individual occurrences. For today it is not rare for such things to be presented as requirements of scientific progress or of a certain new humanism. In numerous places these views are voiced not only in the teachings of philosophers, but on every side they influence literature, the arts, the interpretation of the humanities and of history and civil laws themselves. As a consequence, many people are shaken. . . .

22. The truth is that only in the mystery of the incarnate Word does the mystery of man take on light. For Adam, the first man, was a figure of Him Who was to come, (20) namely Christ the Lord. Christ, the final Adam, by the revelation of the mystery of the Father and His love, fully reveals man to man himself and makes his supreme calling clear. It is not surprising, then, that in Him all the aforementioned truths find their root and attain their crown.

He Who is "the image of the invisible God" (Col. 1:15), (21) is Himself the perfect man. To the sons of Adam He restores the divine likeness which had been disfigured from the first sin onward. Since human nature as He assumed it was not annulled, (22) by that very fact it has been raised up to a divine dignity in our respect too. For by His incarnation the Son of God has united Himself in some fashion with every man. He worked with human hands, He thought with a human mind, acted by human choice (23) and loved with a human heart. Born of the Virgin Mary, He has truly been made one of us, like us in all things except sin. (24)

As an innocent lamb He merited for us life by the free shedding of His own blood. In Him God reconciled us (25) to Himself and among ourselves; from bondage to the devil and sin He delivered us, so that each one of us can say with the Apostle: The Son of God "loved me and gave Himself up for me" (Gal. 2:20). By suffering for us He not only provided us with an example for our imitation, (26) He blazed a trail, and if we follow it, life and death are made holy and take on a new meaning.

The Christian man, conformed to the likeness of that Son Who is the firstborn of many brothers, (27) received "the first-fruits of the Spirit" (Rom. 8:23) by which he becomes capable of discharging the new law of love. (28) Through this Spirit, who is "the pledge of our inheritance" (Eph. 1:14), the whole man is renewed from within, even to the achievement of "the redemption of the body" (Rom. 8:23): "If the Spirit of him who raised Jesus from the death dwells in you, then he who raised Jesus Christ from the dead will also bring to life your mortal bodies because of his Spirit who dwells in you" (Rom. 8:11). (29) Pressing upon the Christian to be sure, are the need and the duty to battle against evil through manifold tribulations and even to suffer death. But, linked with the paschal mystery and patterned on the dying Christ, he will hasten forward to resurrection in the strength which comes from hope. (30)

All this holds true not only for Christians, but for all men of good will in whose hearts grace works in an unseen way. (31) For, since Christ died for all men, (32) and since the ultimate vocation of man is in fact one, and divine, we ought to believe that the Holy Spirit in a manner known only to God offers to every man the possibility of being associated with this paschal mystery.

Such is the mystery of man, and it is a great one, as seen by believers in the light of Christian revelation. Through Christ and in Christ, the riddles of sorrow and death grow meaningful. Apart from His Gospel, they overwhelm us. Christ has risen, destroying death by His death; He has lavished life upon us (33) so that, as sons in the Son, we can cry out in the Spirit; Abba, Father (34)

Chapter 30

The Light of the World:
The Church as the Sacrament of Salvation

Lumen Gentium

Who Wrote It?

No other document produced by the Second Vatican Council underwent such revision from its first draft to its final version than *Lumen Gentium*—the *Dogmatic Constitution on the Church*. The original draft of the document was generated on October 11, 1962, before the Council ever met. But when that document reached the Council members, they demanded that it go in a different direction. The first draft contained anti-Protestant overtones and emphasized the Church as an institution. The final version is known for the way it is based in the sacred Scriptures. *Lumen Gentium* also teaches that the Catholic Church, while possessing the fullness of truth, does not have an exclusive hold on the truth.

When Was It Written?

Lumen Gentium was passed by the Second Vatican Council on November 21, 1964. The final vote was 2,151 for the document and only 5 against it.

Why Was It Written?

Pope John XXIII convened the Second Vatican Council with the intent of setting a new direction for the Church. In no place is that clearer than in *Lumen Gentium*. In this constitution, the bishops laid out the "inner nature and universal mission" of the Church and extended that mission to the whole People of God, not just to the clergy. The document also makes clear that the Church is a pilgrim people, a people destined for everlasting life in Jesus Christ. Because of this destiny, the entire People of God is called to perfect unity and holiness.

Why Is It Still Important Today?

At the time *Lumen Gentium* was written, the idea that all who are baptized share in the universal mission of the Church and that all who are baptized are called to the same perfect unity and holiness as are the ordained and religious was a breathtaking notion. Most Catholics had not been raised to think that way. As radical as it sounded, however, that idea resonated deeply with the Catholic faithful. The image of the Church as a pilgrim people of God is one of the most widely accepted and enduring images of the Council. *Lumen Gentium* can inspire future readers to sustain the mission of the Church and to strive for the universal holiness of the entire People of God that the Lord calls.

Primary Source: *Lumen Gentium*

1. Christ is the Light of nations. Because this is so, this Sacred Synod gathered together in the Holy Spirit eagerly desires, by proclaiming the Gospel to every creature, (1) to bring the light of Christ to all men, a light brightly visible on the countenance of the Church. Since the Church is in Christ like a sacrament or as a sign and instrument both of a very closely knit union with God and of the unity of the whole human race, it desires now to unfold more fully to the faithful of the Church and to the whole world its own inner nature and universal mission. This it intends to do following faithfully the teaching of previous councils. The present-day conditions of the world add greater urgency to this work of the Church so that all men, joined more closely today by various social, technical and cultural ties, might also attain fuller unity in Christ. . . .

    9. At all times and in every race God has given welcome to whosoever fears Him and does what is right. (85) God, however, does not make men holy and save them merely as individuals, without bond or link between one another. Rather has it pleased Him to bring men

together as one people, a people which acknowledges Him in truth and serves Him in holiness. He therefore chose the race of Israel as a people unto Himself. With it He set up a covenant. Step by step He taught and prepared this people, making known in its history both Himself and the decree of His will and making it holy unto Himself. All these things, however, were done by way of preparation and as a figure of that new and perfect covenant, which was to be ratified in Christ, and of that fuller revelation which was to be given through the Word of God Himself made flesh. "Behold the days shall come saith the Lord, and I will make a new covenant with the House of Israel, and with the house of Judah . . . I will give my law in their bowels, and I will write it in their heart, and I will be their God, and they shall be my people . . . For all of them shall know Me, from the least of them even to the greatest, saith the Lord. (86) Christ instituted this new covenant, the new testament, that is to say, in His Blood, (87) calling together a people made up of Jew and gentile, making them one, not according to the flesh but in the Spirit. This was to be the new People of God. For those who believe in Christ, who are reborn not from a perishable but from an imperishable seed through the word of the living God, (88) not from the flesh but from water and the Holy Spirit, (89) are finally established as "a chosen race, a royal priesthood, a holy nation, a purchased people . . . who in times past were not a people, but are now the people of God". (90)

That messianic people has Christ for its head, "Who was delivered up for our sins, and rose again for our justification", (91) and now, having won a name which is above all names, reigns in glory in heaven. The state of this people is that of the dignity and freedom of the sons of God, in whose hearts the Holy Spirit dwells as in His temple. Its law is the new commandment to love as Christ loved us. (92) Its end is the kingdom of God, which has been begun by God Himself on earth, and which is to be further extended until it is brought to perfection by Him at the end of time, when Christ, our life, (93) shall appear, and "creation itself will be delivered from its slavery to corruption into the freedom of the glory of the sons of God". (94) So it is that that messianic people, although it does not actually include all men, and at times may look like a small flock, is nonetheless a lasting and sure seed of unity, hope and salvation for the whole human race. Established by Christ as a communion of life, charity and truth, it is also used by Him as an instrument for the redemption of all, and is sent forth into the whole world as the light of the world and the salt of the earth. (95)

Israel according to the flesh, which wandered as an exile in the desert, was already called the Church of God. (96) So likewise the new Israel which while living in this present age goes in search of a future and abiding city is called the Church of Christ. For He has bought it for Himself with His blood, has filled it with His Spirit and provided it with those means which befit it as a visible and social union. God gathered together as one all those who in faith look upon Jesus as the author of salvation and the source of unity and peace, and established them as the Church that for each and all it may be the visible sacrament of this saving unity. (1*) While it transcends all limits of time and confines of race, the Church is destined to extend to all regions of the earth and so enters into the history of mankind. Moving forward through trial and tribulation, the Church is strengthened by the power of God's grace, which was promised to her by the Lord, so that in the weakness of the flesh she may not waver from perfect fidelity, but remain a bride worthy of her Lord, and moved by the Holy Spirit may never cease to renew herself, until through the Cross she arrives at the light which knows no setting.

10. Christ the Lord, High Priest taken from among men, (100) made the new people "a kingdom and priests to God the Father". (101) The baptized, by regeneration and the anointing of the Holy Spirit, are consecrated as a spiritual house and a holy priesthood, in order that through all those works which are those of the Christian man they may offer spiritual sacrifices and proclaim the power of Him who has called them out of darkness into His marvelous light. (102) Therefore all the disciples of Christ, persevering in prayer and praising God, (103) should present themselves as a living sacrifice, holy and pleasing to God. (104) Everywhere on earth they must bear witness to Christ and give an answer to those who seek an account of that hope of eternal life which is in them. (105)

Though they differ from one another in essence and not only in degree, the common priesthood of the faithful and the ministerial or hierarchical priesthood are nonetheless interrelated: each of them in its own special way is a participation in the one priesthood of Christ. (2*) The ministerial priest, by the sacred power he enjoys, teaches and rules the priestly people; acting in the person of Christ, he makes present the eucharistic sacrifice, and offers it to God in the name of all the people. But the faithful, in virtue of their royal priesthood, join in the offering of the Eucharist. (3*) They likewise exercise that priesthood in receiving the sacraments, in prayer and thanksgiving, in the witness of a holy life, and by self-denial and active charity.

11. It is through the sacraments and the exercise of the virtues that the sacred nature and organic structure of the priestly community is brought into operation. Incorporated in the Church through baptism, the faithful are destined by the baptismal character for the worship of the Christian religion; reborn as sons of God they must confess before men the faith which they have received from God through the Church (4*). They are more perfectly bound to the Church by the sacrament of Confirmation, and the Holy Spirit endows them with special strength so that they are more strictly obliged to spread and defend the faith, both by word and by deed, as true witnesses of Christ (5*). Taking part in the eucharistic sacrifice, which is the fount and apex of the whole Christian life, they offer the Divine Victim to God, and offer themselves along with It (6*). Thus both by reason of the offering and through Holy Communion all take part in this liturgical service, not indeed, all in the same way but each in that way which is proper to himself. Strengthened in Holy Communion by the Body of Christ, they then manifest in a concrete way that unity of the people of God which is suitably signified and wondrously brought about by this most august sacrament.

Those who approach the sacrament of Penance obtain pardon from the mercy of God for the offence committed against Him and are at the same time reconciled with the Church, which they have wounded by their sins, and which by charity, example, and prayer seeks their conversion. By the sacred anointing of the sick and the prayer of her priests the whole Church commends the sick to the suffering and glorified Lord, asking that He may lighten their suffering and save them; (106) she exhorts them, moreover, to contribute to the welfare of the whole people of God by associating themselves freely with the passion and death of Christ. (107) Those of the faithful who are consecrated by Holy Orders are appointed to feed the Church in Christ's name with the word and the grace of God. Finally, Christian spouses, in virtue of the sacrament of Matrimony, whereby they signify and partake of the mystery of that unity and fruitful love which exists between

Christ and His Church, (108) help each other to attain to holiness in their married life and in the rearing and education of their children. By reason of their state and rank in life they have their own special gift among the people of God. (109) (7*) From the wedlock of Christians there comes the family, in which new citizens of human society are born, who by the grace of the Holy Spirit received in baptism are made children of God, thus perpetuating the people of God through the centuries. The family is, so to speak, the domestic church. In it parents should, by their word and example, be the first preachers of the faith to their children; they should encourage them in the vocation which is proper to each of them, fostering with special care vocation to a sacred state.

Fortified by so many and such powerful means of salvation, all the faithful, whatever their condition or state, are called by the Lord, each in his own way, to that perfect holiness whereby the Father Himself is perfect.

Chronological Listing of Chapters

The numbers in the first column represent the year or range of years relevant to each chapter. The second column is the title of the chapter. The third column is the page number for the material in the text.

Topical Index

The scriptural quotations contained herein are from the New Revised Standard Version of the Bible, Catholic Edition. Copyright © 1993 and 1989 by the Division of Christian Education of the National Council of the Churches of Christ in the United States of America. All rights reserved.

Quotations labeled *Catechism* and the material in the sidebar "Filioque: The Holy Spirit 'proceeds from the Father and the Son . . .'" on page 90 (see *Catechism*, paragraphs 243–248) are from the English translation of the *Catechism of the Catholic Church* for use in the United States of America. Copyright © 1994 by the United States Catholic Conference, Inc.—Libreria Editrice Vaticana. Used with permission.

The quotation by Edward Schillebeeckx on page 10 is from *Christ the Sacrament of the Encounter with God,* by Edward Schillebeeckx (Kansas City, MO: Sheed & Ward, 1963), pages 5–6. Copyright © 1963 by Sheed and Ward.

The excerpts in "A Rite of Passage" on pages 12–16 are from "A Rite of Passage," by Aidan Kavanagh, delivered as part of a lecture at the Theology Institute at Holy Cross Abbey in Canon City, Colorado, in August 1977. Used with permission.

The excerpt in "The Dream of Saint John Bosco" on pages 18–20 is from *The Biographical Memoirs of Saint John Bosco,* by Rev. Giovanni Battista Lemoyne, volume 7, 1862–1864 (New Rochelle, NY: Salesiana Publishers, 1972), pages 107–109. Copyright © 1964 by Salesiana. Used with permission.

The excerpts from the *Didache* on pages 34–37, in "Pliny's Questions to the Emperor Trajan Concerning Policy Toward Christians" on pages 39–41, and in "Emperor Trajan's Reply to Pliny's Questions" on pages 41–42 are from *A History of Christianity: Readings in the History of the Church,* volume 1, *The Early and Medieval Church,* edited by Ray Petry (Upper Saddle River, NJ: Prentice-Hall, division of Baker Publishing Group, 1962), pages 13–15, 43–44, and 44, respectively. Copyright © 1962 by Ray C. Petry. Used with permission of Baker Publishing Group.

The words of the doxology on page 35 are from *Catholic Household Blessings and Prayers,* 22. Copyright © 1988 United States Conference of Catholic Bishops, Inc., Washington, DC. All rights reserved.

The excerpts in "The Martyrdom of Saints Perpetua and Felicitas" on pages 44–49 are from *The Acts of the Christian Martyrs,* translated by Herbert Musurillo (Oxford, England: Oxford University Press, 1972), pages 109, 113–115, 117, 125–131. Copyright © 1972 by Oxford University Press. Used with permission of Oxford University Press.

The words of the Edict of Toleration on pages 51–52 and of the Edict of Milan on pages 53–55 are from *Translations and Reprints from the Original Sources of European History,* volume 4, translated by University of Pennsylvania Department of History (Philadelphia: University of Pennsylvania Department of History, 1894–1907), pages 28–30. Copyright © 1894–1907 by University of Pennsylvania Department of History.

The excerpts from *The City of God* on pages 57–61, from *Encyclical Letter to the Archiepiscopal Sees of the East* on pages 90–94, and from "Letters to Pope Gregory XI" on pages 109–111 are from *Readings in Church History,* volume 1, *From Pentecost to the Protestant Revolt,* edited by Colman J. Barry, OSB (Westminster, MD: Newman Press, 1960), pages 130–131, 132–133, and 134; 316–318; and 472–474, respectively. Copyright © 1960 by the Newman Press.

The words of the "Definition of the Faith" on pages 64–68 are from *The Christological Controversy,* translated and edited by Richard Norris Jr. (Philadelphia: Fortress Press, 1980), pages 155–159. Copyright © 1980 by Fortress Press. Used with permission of Augsburg Fortress.

The excerpts in *Ecclesiastical History of the English People* on pages 70–74 are from *Bede: Ecclesiastical History of the English People,* by Wallace-Hadvill, JM (Oxford, England: Oxford University Press, 1988). Copyright © 1988 by Wallace-Hadvill, JM. Used with permission of Oxford University Press.

The words of Pope Saint Gregory the Great in "Letter to Abbot Mellitus" on pages 74–75 are from "Gregory I: Letter to Abbot Mellitus Epistola 76, PL 77: 1215-1216" at *www.fordham.edu/halsall/source/greg1-mellitus.txt,* accessed December 8, 2004.

The quotation in the "Hospitality" sidebar on page 77 and the words from the prologue to *The Rule of St. Benedict* on pages 78–80 are from *The Rule of St. Benedict,* translated by Anthony Meisel and M. L.

Del Mastro (New York: Image Book, Doubleday, 1975), pages 43–45 and 89. Copyright © 1975 by Anthony Meisel and M. L. Del Mastro. Used with permission of Doubleday, a division of Random House.

The excerpts in "Letter Advising Saint Boniface on How to Convert the Heathens" on pages 82–83 and in "Report to Pope Zacharias on the Foundation of Fulda Abbey" on pages 85–87 are from "Letters of Saint Boniface to the Popes and Others," by George Washington Robinson, in *Papers of the American Society of Church History,* second series, by American Society of Church History (New York: G. P. Putnam's Sons, 1889-1934), pages vi and 157–186. Copyright © 1888 by G. P. Putnam's Sons.

The excerpts in "Correspondence Regarding Lay Investiture" on pages 96–101 and in "Letters from a Nazi Prison" on pages 170–173 are from *A Cloud of Witnesses: Readings in the History of Western Christianity,* revised edition, edited by Joel F. Harrington (New York: Houghton Mifflin, 2001), pages 134–136 and 473–474. Copyright © 2001 by Houghton Mifflin Company. Reprinted with permission.

The excerpts in "The Testament of Saint Francis" on pages 103–106 are from *The Writings of St. Francis of Assisi,* translated from the Critical Latin Edition, edited by Fr. Kajetan Esser, OFM. A publication of the The Franciscan Archive, 2000, at *www.franciscan-archive.org/patriarcha/opera/dictata.html,* accessed December 8, 2004.

The excerpt in *The Imitation of Christ* on pages 113–116 is adapted from *The Imitation of Christ* by Thomas á Kempis (New York: Macmillan, 1940), pages 83–90. Copyright © 1910 by Macmillan Company.

The excerpt in "Writings from Martin Luther" on pages 119–121 is from "An Introduction to St. Paul's Letter to the Romans" in *Luther's German Bible of 1522,* by Martin Luther, translated by Rev. Robert E. Smith from *Dr. Martin Luther's Vermischte Deutsche Schriften,* volume 63, edited by Johann K. Irmischer (Erlangen, Germany: Heyder and Zimmer, 1854), pages 124–125, at *www.iclnet.org/pub/resources/text/wittenberg/luther/luther-faith.txt.*

The excerpts from *The Way of Perfection* on pages 124–126 are from *The Collected Works of St. Teresa of Avila,* volume 2, translated by Kieran Kavanaugh and Otilio Rodriquez (Washington, DC: ICS Publications, 1980), pages 41–43 and 47–48. Copyright © 1980 by Washington Province of Discalced Carmelites, ICS Publications, 2131 Lincoln Road, NE, Washington, DC 20002 U.S.A., *www.icspublications.org.* Used with permission.

The excerpt from the "Declaration of Vision: Toward the Next 500 Years" statement to the 1993 Parliament of the World's Religions on page 128 is from *Turtle Quarterly*, Fall-Winter 1994, page 8, at *www.ili.nativeweb.org/dovision.html*, accessed December 9, 2004.

The excerpts from *Inter Caetera* on pages 128–130 are from The Catholic Community Forum at *www.catholic-forum.com/saints/pope0214a.htm*, accessed December 8, 2004.

The quotation from "Declaration on the Relation of the Church to Non-Christian Religions" on page 131 is from *www.vatican.va/roman_curia/secretariat state/2004/documents/rc_seg-st_20040914_osce-brussels_en.html*, accessed December 7, 2004.

The excerpt from *Sublimus Dei* on pages 131–132 is from Papal Encyclicals Online at *www.papalencyclicals.net/Paul03/p3subli.htm*, accessed December 8, 2004.

The quotation on page 134 is from the "Message of Pope John Paul II to the Participants in the International Conference Commemorating the Fourth Centenary of the Arrival in Beijing of Father Matteo Ricci" at *www.vatican.va/holy_father/john_paul_ii/speeches/2001/october/documents/hf_jp-ii_spe_20011024_matteo-ricci_en.html*, accessed December 7, 2004.

The excerpt in "Letter to Francesco Pasio, SJ, Vice-Provincial of China and Japan" on pages 134–137 is from *Readings in Church History*, volume 2, *The Reformation and the Absolute States 1517–1789*, edited by Colman J. Barry (Westminster, MD: Newman Press, 1967), pages 222–224. Copyright © 1965 by The Missionary Society of Saint Paul and the Apostle in the State of New York.

The excerpts on pages 139–143 are from *Rerum Novarum*, an encyclical of Pope Leo XIII on capital and labor, at *www.vatican.va/holy_father/leo_xiii/encyclicals/documents/hf_l-xiii_enc_15051891_rerum-novarum_en.html*, accessed December 8, 2004.

The excerpts from *Pastor Æternus* on pages 145–149 are from *Decrees of the Ecumenical Councils*, volume 2, edited by Norman Tanner (London: Sheed & Ward Limited; Washington, DC: Georgetown University Press, 1990), pages 800, 811–812, 812, 813, 814–815, 815–816. Text copyright © 1972 by Instituto per le scienze religiose, Bologna. English translation copyright © 1990 by Sheed & Ward Limited and the Trustees for Roman Catholic Purposes Registered.

The excerpts in "Report on the Mission of San Carlos de Monterey" on pages 151–155 and in "A Letter to the Society for the Propagation of the Faith" on pages 157–161 are from *Documents of American Catholic History,* volume 1, edited by John Tracy Ellis (Wilmington, DE: Michael Glazier, 1987), pages 34–36 and 43–45 and 222–224, 326–329. Copyright © 1987 by John Tracy Ellis.

The excerpts in *The Long Loneliness* on pages 163–168 are from *The Long Loneliness,* by Dorothy Day (NY: Harper & Row Publishers, 1980), pages 204–206, 212–213, 215, and 221–222. Copyright © 1952 by Harper & Row Publishers. Copyright renewed © 1980 by Tamar Teresa Hennessey. Used with permission of Harper Collins, Inc.

The quotation on page 170 is from "The Peace Pulpit," by Bishop Thomas J. Gumbleton, *National Catholic Reporter,* March 2, 2003, at *www.nationalcatholicreporter.org/peace/gumb0302.htm,* accessed December 9, 2004.

The quotation from Pope John Paul II on page 175 is from the encyclical *Dives in misericordia,* paragraph 12, at *www.vatican.va/holy_father/john_paul_ii/encyclicals/documents/hf_jp-ii_enc_30111980_dives-in-misericordia_en.html,* accessed December 6, 2004.

The excerpts from *Gaudium et Spes* on pages 176–178 are from *www.vatican.va/archive/hist_councils/ii_vatican_council/documents/vat-ii_cons_19651207_gaudium-et-spes_en.html,* accessed September 24, 2004.

The quotation on page 180 and the excerpts from *Lumen Gentium* on pages 180–184 are from *www.vatican.va/archive/hist_councils/ii_vatican_council/documents/vat-ii_const_19641121_lumen-gentium_en.html,* accessed December 9, 2004.

To view copyright terms and conditions for Internet materials cited here, log on to the home pages for the referenced Web sites.

During this book's preparation, all citations, facts, figures, names, addresses, telephone numbers, Internet URLs, and other pieces of information cited within were verified for accuracy. The authors and Saint Mary's Press staff have made every attempt to reference current and valid sources, but we cannot guarantee the content of any source, and we are not responsible for any changes that may have occurred since our verification. If you find an error in, or have a question or concern about, any of the information or sources listed within, please contact Saint Mary's Press.